Magic Lantern Guides®

Canon
EOS
REBEL T1i
EOS 500D

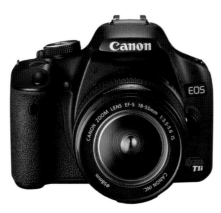

Michael Guncheon

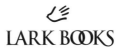

LARK BOOKS

A Division of Sterling Publishing Co., Inc.
New York / London

Editor: K. Helmkamp
Book Design: Michael Robertson
Cover Design: Thom Gaines – Electron Graphics

Library of Congress Cataloging-in-Publication Data

Guncheon, Michael A., 1959-
  Canon EOS T1i/EOS 500D / Michael Guncheon. -- 1st ed.
      p. cm. -- (Magic lantern guides)
  Includes index.
  ISBN 978-1-60059-610-0 (pbk. : alk. paper)
  1. Canon digital cameras--Handbooks, manuals, etc. 2. Digital cameras--Handbooks, manuals, etc.
3. Photography--Digital techniques--Handbooks, manuals, etc. 4. Single lens reflex cameras--
Handbooks, manuals, etc. I. Title.
  TR263.C3.G973 2009
  771.3'3--dc22
                                        2009021370

10 9 8 7 6 5 4 3 2 1
First Edition

Published by Lark Books, A Division of
Sterling Publishing Co., Inc.
387 Park Avenue South, New York, N.Y. 10016

Text © 2010, Michael Guncheon
Photography © 2010, Michael Guncheon unless otherwise specified

Distributed in Canada by Sterling Publishing,
c/o Canadian Manda Group, 165 Dufferin Street
Toronto, Ontario, Canada M6K 3H6

Distributed in the United Kingdom by GMC Distribution Services,
Castle Place, 166 High Street, Lewes, East Sussex, England BN7 1XU

Distributed in Australia by Capricorn Link (Australia) Pty Ltd.,
P.O. Box 704, Windsor, NSW 2756 Australia

This book is not sponsored by Canon.

If you have questions or comments about this book, please contact:
Lark Books
67 Broadway
Asheville, NC 28801
(828) 253-0467

Manufactured in Canada

ISBN 13: 978-1-60059-610-0

For information about custom editions, special sales, premium and corporate purchases, please contact
Sterling Special Sales Department at 800-805-5489 or specialsales@sterlingpub.com.

Contents

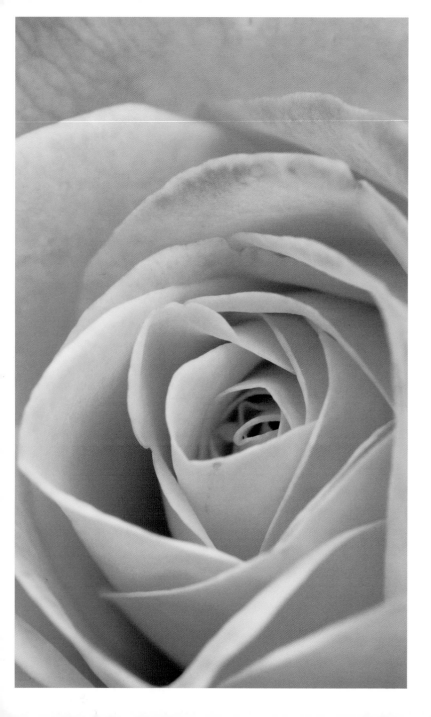

Digital Photography:
The Revolution Continues

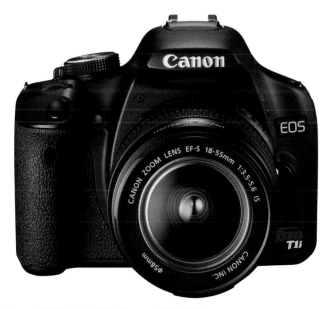

Canon EOS Rebel T1i / Canon EOS 500D

Back in 2003 Canon started the affordable digital SLR revolution with the original EOS Digital Rebel. For the first time, photographers could buy a digital SLR (D-SLR) for under $1,000 US. Since then Canon has continued to introduce new Rebels, each with higher image quality and better features than its predecessor. Less than a year after the last Rebel was introduced, Canon has created the EOS Rebel T1i, also known as the EOS 500D outside North America. With its introduction, Canon has continued to set the standard for affordable digital SLRs.

The Canon EOS Rebel T1i provides professional-quality images from a large 15.1 MP sensor and video capabilities at a more affordable price-point than the Canon EOS 5D Mark II.

13

Introduced in March of 2009, the T1i's body measures only 5.1 x 3.8 x 2.4 inches (128.8 x 97.5 x 61.9 mm) and weighs just 16.9 ounces (480 g) without lens. Yet the Rebel T1i offers a newly developed 15.1 megapixel image sensor, as well as additional features that compare favorably with cameras that come with a much higher price tag.

The new sensor incorporates improved circuitry and an advanced color filter that increases sensitivity and improves color fidelity. A key feature of this new CMOS sensor is low power consumption, enabling you to record HD video through the Live View shooting feature.

At the heart of the image processing circuitry is a brand new DIGIC 4 image processor. This special chip is the latest in a long line of Canon-designed image processors. The DIGIC 4 provides even faster image processing and higher sensitivity with lower noise performance, than ever before.

Some photographers have purchased the Rebel T1i as an upgrade from the EOS Digital Rebel, Rebel XT, Rebel XTi, Rebel XS, or Rebel XSi. Others, however, are making their first high-quality digital camera investment. For those photographers new to digital SLR photography, this book begins with an assortment of basic topics and concepts. Experienced digital photographers and anyone already familiar with these terms and concepts should skip ahead to the detailed sections on camera operation, beginning on page 119.

As a matter of convenience (and easier reading), I usually refer to the Canon EOS Rebel T1i simply as the Rebel T1i. As previously mentioned, outside of North America the same camera is known as the Canon EOS 500D. Operationally the cameras are identical and this guide can be used for both.

Canon created the multi-featured Rebel T1i to meet the requirements of photographers of all levels of experience. While this book thoroughly explores all of the Rebel T1i's features, you certainly don't need to know how to operate every one. Once you understand what a feature does, you

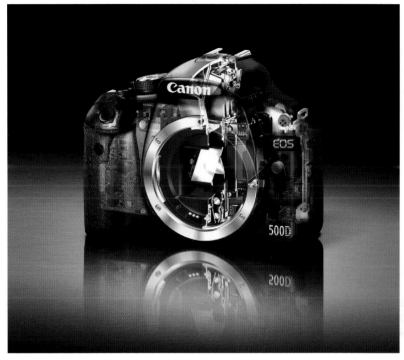

The DIGIC 4 image processor improves the Rebel T1i's performance by providing better noise reduction, faster image recording, and more accurate image color.

may decide it is not necessary to master it in order to achieve your desired photographic results. Learn the basic controls. Explore any additional features that work for you. Forget the rest. At some point in the future you can always delve further into this book and work to develop your Rebel T1i techniques and skills. Just remember that the best time to learn about a feature is before you need it.

Digital cameras do some things differently than traditional film cameras, making them exciting and fun to use, no matter whether you are an amateur or a pro. For digital beginners, many of these differences may seem complicated or confusing. Though most of the features found on a traditional Canon film camera are also available on the Rebel T1i, there are many new controls and operations unique to digital. Other features have been added to increase the camera's versatility for different shooting styles and requirements. The goal of this guide is to help you understand how the camera operates so that you can choose the techniques that work best for you and your style of photography.

Differences between
Digital and Film Photography

Just a few years ago it was easy to tell the difference between photos taken with a digital camera and those shot with a traditional film camera: Pictures from digital cameras didn't measure up in quality. This is no longer true. When you shoot with the Rebel T1i, you can make prints of at least 16 x 20 inches (40.6 x 50.8 cm) that will match an enlargement from 35mm film.

Although there are differences between film and digital image capture, there are many similarities as well. A camera is basically a box that holds a lens that focuses light onto a light-sensitive frame, or medium. In traditional photography, the light-sensitive frame is a piece of film that is later developed with chemicals. In digital photography, however, the frame is the image sensor that converts the light to voltages. The camera then converts the voltages into digital data that represents the pixels that make up an image. In essence, unlike a film camera, a digital camera "develops" the image within the camera.

Film vs. the Sensor

Both film and digital cameras expose pictures using virtually identical methods. The light metering systems are based on the same technologies. The sensitivity standards for both film and sensors are similar, and the shutter and aperture mechanisms are basically the same. These similarities exist because both film and digital cameras share the same function: to deliver the amount of light required by the sensitized medium to create a picture you will like.

However, image sensors react to light differently than film does. From dark areas (such as navy blue blazers, asphalt, and shadows) to midtones (blue sky and green grass) to bright areas (such as white houses and snowy slopes), a digital sensor responds to the full range of light equally, or linearly. Film, however, responds linearly only to midtones. Therefore, film blends tones very well in highlight areas, whereas digital sensors often cut out at the brightest tones. Digital typically responds to highlights in the way that slide film does, and to shadows as does print film.

The LCD Monitor

One of the major limitations of film is that you really don't know if your picture is a success until the film is developed. You have to wait to find out if the exposure was correct or if something happened to spoil the results (such as the blurring of a moving subject or stray reflections from flash). The Rebel T1i features a new large LCD monitor (3 inches; 7.6 cm) with higher resolution so you can review your image within seconds of taking the shot. Though you may not be able to see all the minute details on this small screen, the display provides a general idea of what has been recorded, so you can evaluate your pictures as soon as you shoot them.

The Histogram

Whether you shoot film or digital, the wrong exposure causes problems. Digital cameras do not offer any magic that lets you beat the laws of physics: Too little light makes dark images; too much makes overly bright images. Just looking at the image on the LCD monitor will not help you evaluate exposure. Fortunately, the LCD monitor can display an exposure graph, or histogram, which gives an essentially instantaneous look at your exposure. At first this graph may seem confusing, but after you learn how to read it (page 134) you'll soon realize that it is one of the most powerful tools in digital photography.

With traditional film, many photographers regularly bracket exposures (shoot the same image several times while changing settings, e.g. increasing or decreasing shutter speed or aperture on consecutive shots) in order to ensure they get the exposure they want. You can still bracket with digital if you want—the T1i can do it automatically for you—but there is less of a need because you can check your exposure using the histogram as you shoot.

Film vs. Memory Cards
Images captured by a digital camera are stored on memory cards. These removable cards affect photographic technique by offering the following advantages over film:

More photos: Standard 35mm film comes in two sizes: 24 and 36 exposures. Memory cards come in a range of capacities, and all but the smallest are capable of holding more exposures than film (depending on the selected file type).

Reusable: Once you make an exposure with film, you have to develop and store the negative and print. Due to a chemical reaction, the emulsion layer is permanently changed, so the film cannot be reused. With a memory card, you can remove images at any time, opening space for additional photos. This simplifies the process of organizing your final set of images. Once images are transferred to your computer (or other storage medium—burning a CD is recommended), the card can be reused.

Durability: Memory cards are much more durable than film. They can be removed from the camera at any time (as long as the camera is turned off) without the risk of ruined pictures. They can even be taken through the carry-on inspection machines at the airport without suffering damage.

No ISO limitations: Digital cameras can be set to record at different light sensitivities, or ISO speeds, at any time. This means the card is able to capture images using different ISO settings, even on a picture-by-picture basis. With film, you must expose the entire roll before you can change sensitivity.

Small size: In the space taken up by just a couple rolls of film, you can store or carry multiple memory cards that will hold hundreds of images.

Greater image permanence: The latent image on exposed, but undeveloped, film is susceptible to degradation due to conditions such as heat and humidity. With new security precautions at airports, the potential for film damage has increased. But digital photography allows greater peace of mind. Not only are memory cards durable, their images can also be easily downloaded to storage devices or laptops. This flexibility comes with a risk—the chance that images may be inadvertently erased—so make sure you make backups.

ISO

ISO is an international standard method for quantifying film's sensitivity to light. Once an ISO number is assigned to a film, you can count on its having a standard sensitivity, or speed, regardless of the manufacturer. Low numbers, such as 50 or 100, represent a relatively low sensitivity, and films with these speeds are called slow films. Films with high numbers, such as 400 or above, are more sensitive and are referred to as fast. ISO numbers are mathematically proportional to the sensitivity to light. As you double or halve the ISO number, you double or halve the film's sensitivity to light (i.e. 800 speed film is twice as sensitive to light as 400 speed, and it is half as sensitive to light as 1600 speed).

Technically, digital cameras do not have a true ISO. The sensor has a specific sensitivity to light. Its associated circuits change its relative "sensitivity" by amplifying the signal from the chip. For practical purposes, however, the ISO setting on a digital camera corresponds to film. If you set a digital camera to ISO 400, you can expect a response to light that is similar to ISO 400 film.

Unlike film, changing ISO picture-by-picture is easy with a digital camera. By merely changing the ISO setting, you use the sensor's electronics to change its sensitivity. It's like changing film at the touch of a button. This capability provides many advantages. For example, you could be indoors using an ISO setting of 800 so you don't need flash, and then you can follow your subject outside into direct sunlight and change to ISO 100. The Rebel T1i D-SLR offers an extremely wide range of ISO settings, from 100 to 3,200, that can be expanded to 100-12,800.

With the new image sensor and the DIGIC 4 image processing chip, the Rebel T1i has very low noise when used at high ISO settings. This means that you can use a higher ISO than you would with any other Digital Rebel.

Noise and Grain
Noise in digital photography is the equivalent of grain in film photography. It appears as an irregular, sand-like texture that can be unsightly at worst and essentially invisible at best. (As with grain, this fine-patterned look is sometimes desirable for certain creative effects.) In film, grain occurs due to the chemical structure of the light-sensitive materials. In digital cameras, noise occurs for several reasons: sensor noise (caused by various things, including heat from the electronics and optics), digital artifacts (when digital technology cannot deal with fine tonalities such as sky gradations), and JPEG artifacts (caused by image compression). Of all of these, sensor noise is the most common.

In both film and digital photography, grain or noise emerges when using high ISO speeds. On any camera, noise is more obvious with underexposure. With digital cameras, noise may also increase with long exposures in low-light conditions. The Rebel T1i's new sensor gathers more light and has improved noise reduction circuitry to minimize digital noise. This technology gives the camera incredible image quality—even at high ISOs—that simply wasn't possible in the past. This camera also has a number of technologies that create better images with long exposures.

File Formats
A digital camera converts the continuous (or analog) image information from the sensor into digital data. The data may be saved into either of two different digital file formats, RAW or JPEG.

One very useful feature of digital SLRs is their ability to capture a RAW file. RAW files are image files that include information about how the image was shot but that have little processing applied by the camera. They also contain 14-bit color information, which is the maximum amount of data available from the sensor. (It is a little confusing that the RAW file format is actually a 16-bit file, though the data from the sensor is 14-bit.) The Rebel T1i uses Canon's proprietary RAW file, the CR2 file—the same advanced RAW format developed for the Canon EOS-1D Mark II.

JPEG (Joint Photographic Experts Group) is a standard format for image compression and is the most common file created by digital cameras. Digital cameras use this format because it reduces the size of the file, allowing more pictures to fit on a memory card. It is highly optimized for photographic images.

Both RAW and JPEG files can produce excellent results. The unprocessed data of a RAW file can be helpful when you are faced with tough exposure situations, but the small size of the JPEG file is faster and easier to deal with. It is important to consider that a JPEG image might look great right out of the camera, while a RAW file may need quite a bit of adjustment before the image looks good. When in doubt, the T1i offers the option of recording both RAW and JPEG files of each image.

Digital Resolution

When we talk about resolution in film, we refer to the level of detail that the film can see or distinguish. Similarly, when referring to resolution in the context of lenses, we measure the lens' ability to separate elements of detail in a subject. With digital cameras, however, resolution indicates the number of individual pixels that are contained on the imaging sensor. This is usually expressed in megapixels. Each pixel captures a portion of the total light falling on the sensor. And it is from these pixels that the image is created. Thus, a 15-megapixel camera has 15 million pixels covering the sensor.

Dealing with Resolution: The Rebel T1i offers three different resolution settings from 3.7 to 15.1 megapixels. Although you don't always have to choose the camera's maximum resolution, generally it is best to use the highest setting available (i.e., get the most detail possible with your camera). You can always reduce resolution in the computer, but you cannot recreate detail if you never captured the data to begin with. Keep in mind that you paid for the megapixels in your camera! The lower the resolution with which you choose to shoot, the less detail your picture will have. This is particularly noticeable when making enlargements. The Rebel T1i has the potential of making great prints at 16 x 20 inches (40.6 x 50.8 cm) and larger, but only when the image is shot at 15.1 megapixels.

Digital camera files generally enlarge very well in image editing programs, especially if you recorded them in RAW format first. (Recall that there is more data with which to work in the RAW format.) The higher the original shooting resolution, the larger the print you can make. However, if the photos are specifically for email or webpage use, you do not need to shoot with a high resolution in order for the images to look good on screen.

Remember, you can always reduce the resolution later in the computer. But you can't increase resolution without producing digital artifacts.

The Color of Light

Anyone who has shot color slide film in a variety of lighting conditions has horror stories about the color resulting from those conditions. Color reproduction is affected by how a film is "balanced" or matched to the color of the light. Our eyes adapt to the differences, but film does not.

In practical terms, if you shoot a daylight-balanced (outdoor) film while indoors under incandescent lights, your image will have an orange cast to it. For accurate color reproduction in this instance, you would need to change the film or use a color correction filter. One of the toughest popular lights to balance is fluorescent. The type and age of the bulbs affect their color and how that color appears on film, usually requiring careful filtration. Though filters are helpful in altering and correcting the color of light, they also darken the viewfinder, increase the exposure, and make it harder to focus and compose the image.

With digital cameras, all of this changed. A digital camera acts more like our eyes and it creates images with fewer color problems. This is because color correction is managed by the white balance function. White balance is an internal setting built into all digital cameras, allowing them to use electronic circuits to neutralize whites and other neutral colors, without using filters. This technology can automatically check the light and calculate the proper setting for the light's color temperature. White balance can also be set to specific light conditions, or custom-set for any number of possible conditions. Thanks to this technology, filters are rarely a necessity for color correction, making color casts and light loss a non-issue.

Cost of Shooting

While film cameras have traditionally cost less than digital cameras, an interesting phenomenon is taking place that makes a digital camera a better overall value. Memory cards have become quite affordable. Once a card is purchased, it can be used again and again. Therefore, the cost per image decreases as the use of the card increases. Conversely, the more pictures you take with film, the more rolls you have to buy (and process), and the more expensive the photography becomes.

With digital cameras there is virtually no cost to shooting a large number of photos. The camera and memory card are already paid for, whether one, ten, or a hundred images are shot. This can be liberating because photographers can now try new ways of shooting, experiment with creative angles never attempted before, and so much more.

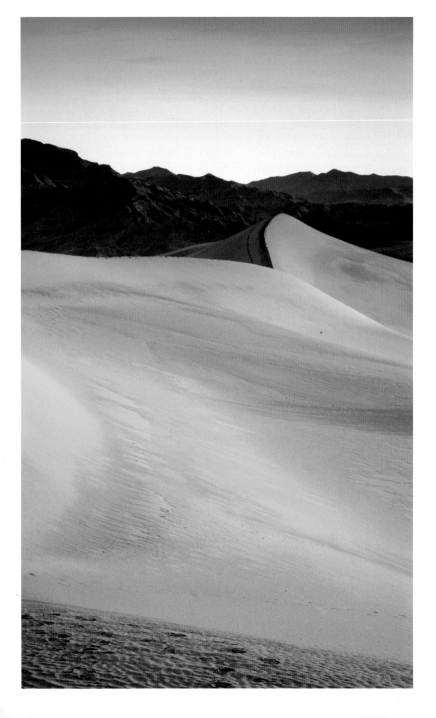

Features and Functions

Today's digital cameras offer a dizzying array of features in order to appeal to a broad spectrum of buyers. You may find you do not need or will not use all of them. This book explains all the features on the Rebel T1i, and helps you master those that are most important to you. Don't feel guilty if you don't use every option packed into the camera. On the other hand, remember that you can't "waste film" with digital cameras. Shoot as much as you want and then erase those images that don't work. This means you can literally try out every feature on your camera to see how it functions. This is a quick and sure way of learning to use your camera, and it helps you determine which features really are most useful to you.

The Canon EOS Rebel T1i offers a high degree of technological sophistication at an affordable price. In many ways, it sets the bar for all other digital SLRs (D-SLRs) in this price range. With a sensor that contains 15.1 megapixels (MP), the Rebel T1i shoots 3.4 frames per second (fps) and up to 170 JPEG or 9 RAW frames consecutively. It also offers quick start-up, fast memory card writing speeds, and other controls that match the performance of many top pro cameras.

The chassis of the T1i is constructed using stainless steel, which makes the camera able to stand up to years of use. The camera is housed in a specially engineered polycarbonate body. While more expensive to manufacture, this construction creates a lightweight, yet strong, unit. The exterior of the camera is ergonomically designed and textured to provide for a solid grip.

The first step to taking great photos with the Rebel T1i is to familiarize yourself with the camera's features and functions and how to access and control them.

Canon has used its EF-S lens mount for this camera. Introduced with the original Digital Rebel (EOS 300D), this mount accepts all standard Canon EF lenses. In addition, it accepts compact EF-S lenses, built specifically for small-format sensors. EF-S lenses can only be used on cameras designed expressly to accept them.

One of the biggest changes to the camera compared to previous Rebels is the LCD monitor on the back of the camera. The T1i is the first Rebel to include the high-resolution 3-inch (7.62 cm) display found on Canon's professional cameras.

Note: When the terms "left" and "right" are used to describe the locations of camera controls, it is assumed that the camera is being held in horizontal shooting position.

Overview of Features

- Canon-designed and Canon-built 15.1 MP, small-format, APS-C sized CMOS sensor.

- High definition video recording, 1920x1080 at 20 fps (progressive) recording and 1280x720 at 30fps (progressive) recording, and standard definition, all with audio from a built-in microphone.

- DIGIC 4 image processor for high-speed, low-noise performance.

- 14-bit analog-to-digital conversion for improved RAW file quality, and enhanced JPEG conversion.

- New, larger, brighter, and sharper 3 inch (7.62 cm) high-resolution color display with anti-reflective and scratch-resistant coatings, and automatic brightness control.

- Shoots 3.4 fps and up to 170 frames consecutively at maximum JPEG resolution (9 frames continuous in RAW and 4 shots RAW+JPEG).

- ISO range of 100-3,200 extendable to 100-12,800.

- Live View shooting mode with Face Detection AF.

- Integrated sensor cleaning system and Canon "Dust Delete Data" detection.

- Fast shutter lag time (about 0.09 seconds) and viewfinder black-out time (approx. 130ms at speeds 1/60th and higher).

- 6 preset Picture Style settings and 3 user-defined custom Picture Style settings.

- High-speed focal plane shutter – up to 1/4000 second – with flash sync up to 1/200 second.

- 9-point autofocus system.

- Easy access to AF (autofocus) points, menus, and other features via cross key system.

- Quick Control Screen provides fast access to camera settings without going into menus.

- User-activated noise subtraction for long exposures.

- High ISO noise reduction.

- Auto lighting optimizer for automatic adjustment of scene brightness and contrast.

- Lens peripheral illumination correction for automatic compensation of light fall-off at the corners of the image.

- Fully compatible with entire EOS system of lenses, flash, and other accessories.

- Flexible file numbering system.

- Power-saving design promotes longer battery life.

Canon EOS Rebel T1i – Front View

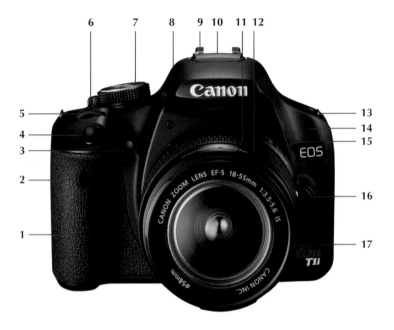

1. Grip
2. Remote control sensor
3. Red eye reduction /
   Self-timer lamp
4. Shutter button
5. Main dial
6. Power switch
7. Mode Dial
8. Built-in flash /
   AF-assist beam

9. Hot shoe
10. Flash-sync contacts
11. EF Lens mount index
12. EF-S Lens mount index
13. Strap mount
14. Microphone
15. Flash button
16. Lens release button
17. Depth-of-field preview
    button

Canon EOS Rebel T1i – Rear View

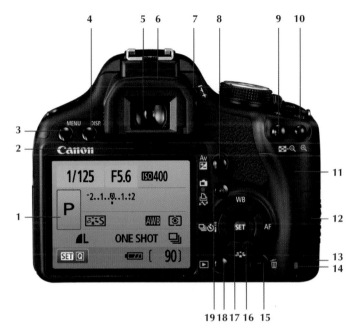

1. LCD monitor
2. Display-off sensor
3. Menu button
4. Shooting settings display button
5. Viewfinder eyepiece
6. Eyecup
7. Dioptric adjustment knob
8. Aperture / Exposure compensation button
9. AE lock / FE lock button / Index / Reduce button
10. AF point selection / Magnify button
11. Speaker
12. Card slot cover
13. DC cord hole
14. Access lamp
15. Erase button
16. Cross keys:
    Up: White Balance selection button
    Down: Picture style selection button
    Left: Drive mode selection button
    Right: AF mode selection button
17. Setting button
18. Playback button
19. Live View shooting / Movie shooting / Print / Share button

Canon EOS Rebel T1i – Top View

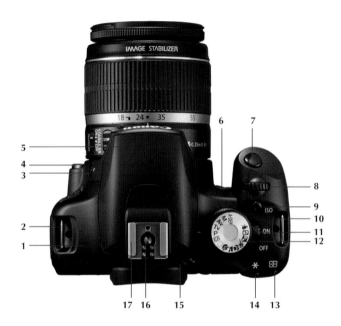

1. Focal plane mark
2. Strap mount
3. Flash button
4. Lens release button
5. Built-in flash /
   AF-assist beam
6. Red-eye reduction /
   Self-time lamp
7. Shutter button
8. Main Dial
9. ISO speed setting button

10. Strap mount
11. Power switch
12. Mode Dial
13. AF point selection /
    Magnify button
14. AE lock / FE lock button /
    Index / Reduce button
15. Dioptric adjustment knob
16. Flash-sync contacts
17. Hot shoe

Camera Controls

The EOS Rebel T1i uses icons, buttons, and dials common to all Canon cameras. Specific buttons are explained with the features they control. The Rebel T1i often uses two controls to manage the most common and important functions.

Mode Dial ◉

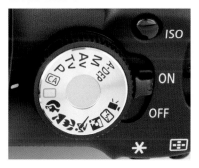

Located on top of the camera next to the power switch, the Mode dial is used to select various shooting modes. These settings are grouped into two zones: Basic Zone and Creative Zone. The Basic Zone has a subset of settings called the Image Zone. You can think of this as a "scene" mode similar to those found on point-and-shoot cameras. In addition to the 12 shooting settings is a setting for shooting movies.

Main Dial ⌒

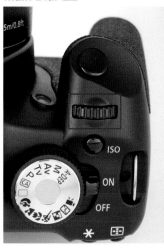

Behind the shutter button on the top right of the camera is the Main dial. It allows you to use your shooting finger to set things like exposure. The Main dial works alone when setting shutter speed and aperture. For a number of other adjustments, it works in conjunction with buttons that are either pressed and released, or are held down while the Main dial is turned.

Shutter Button

The Rebel T1i features a soft-touch electromagnetic shutter release. Partially depressing it activates such functions as autoexposure and autofocus, but this camera is fast enough that there is minimal speed in doing this. However, when you deal with moving subjects it helps to start autofocusing early, so the camera and lens have time to find your subject.

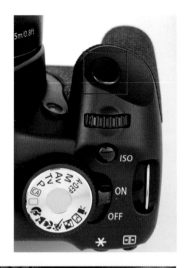

Cross Keys ✧

The cross keys aid in menu navigation as well as allowing instant access to certain camera settings, such as white balance.

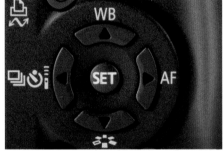

These four keys, arranged in a cross pattern with a centered Set button ⑤, are located on the back of the camera to the right of the LCD monitor. As a group, the keys control navigation by allowing you to scroll up/down and left/right through menus. In addition, each key allows quick access to a specific menu item. When the camera is set for picture taking, individual keys provide instant access to AF mode ▶ AF, Picture Style selection ▼ ♣❖, drive mode settings ◀❑/❖, and white balance settings ▲ WB. When Live View shooting is enabled, the ⑤ button must be pressed to access the cross keys. The Set button is also used to access the Quick Control Screen. ⑤ can also be programmed for various options using Custom Function C.Fn-11 (see page 79).

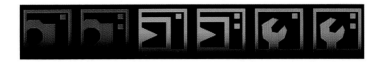

Menus Overview

The Rebel T1i has several menus for capturing and viewing images, as well as setting up the operation of the camera. Once you press MENU, located on the back of the camera above the left corner of the LCD monitor, the menus display on the LCD monitor. The menu structure consists of eight menu tabs. (See pages 65-72 for more details about the T1i menus).

The first two tabs, color-coded red, are Shooting Menus 1 and 2: ◻' and ◻'. They deal with image capturing functions. The third and fourth tabs, color-coded blue, are the Playback Menus – ⊒' and ⊒' – which allow you to adjust the LCD's image display options and control image transfer and printing. The next three tabs, color-coded yellow, are Set-up Menus 1, 2, and 3: ϔ', ϔ', and ϔ'. These deal with a variety of camera set-up functions. The last tab is the green color-coded My Menu 🗗, enabling you to build your own set of options, customizing the T1i for your personal shooting needs. Once you have pressed MENU, navigate through the menu tabs by using the Main dial 🖦 or the left/right cross keys ◀▶.

If you are in one of the Basic Zone's shooting modes (see page 137), the Shooting 2 ◻', Set-up 3 ϔ', and My Menu 🗗 menu tabs, as well as a few specific menu items, will not be available. If you can't find a menu item or it is grayed out, check to see if the camera is in one of the Basic Zone's shooting modes.

33

When the camera is in movie shooting mode (the Mode dial ⊙ is set for '🎥) an additional menu tab appears to the left of the first Shooting Menu tab ◘. This menu '🎥 gives access to specific settings used during video recording, including movie size, grid display, and sound recording.

Note: When adjusting settings in the menus, be sure to press the Set button ⊛, located in the center of the cross keys ✧, to accept [OK] the setting; otherwise the T1i reverts to the earlier setting.

Camera Activation

Power Switch
The power switch is found on the top right of the camera next to the Mode dial ⊙. When set to the [ON] position, the camera operates as long as the battery contains a charge.

Auto Power Off

The Auto power off control can save the T1i's battery power if the camera remains idle for a period of time.

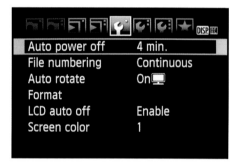

All digital cameras automatically shut off after a period of inactivity to conserve power. The Rebel T1i has an Auto power off selection in the Set-up 1 menu ❡ that can be used to turn off the power after a period of idleness. To turn the camera back on, simply press the shutter button.

Auto power off is helpful to minimize battery use, but you may find it frustrating if you try to take a picture and find that the camera has shut itself off. For example, you might be shooting a basketball game and the action may stay away from you for a couple of minutes. If Auto power off is set to [30 sec.], the camera may be off as the players move toward you. When you try to shoot, nothing will happen because the camera is powering back up. You may miss the important shot. In this case, you might want to change the setting to [4 min.] or [8 min.] so the camera stays on when you need it.

Access the Auto power off function through the camera's menus. Press **MENU** and advance to the ✌ menu (color code yellow) using the Main dial ✍. When the ✌ menu is highlighted, use the up/down cross keys ▲▼ to highlight [Auto power off]—the first option in this menu—and press ⑳. You are given seven different choices, ranging from 30 seconds to 15 minutes (including the [Off] option that prevents the camera from turning off automatically). Scroll with the cross keys to highlight the desired duration and press ⑳ to select it.

Resetting Controls

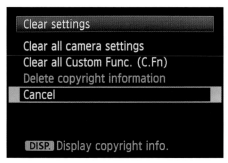

It is easy to reset the camera controls with this menu selection.

With all the controls built into the Rebel T1i, it is possible to set so many combinations that at some point you may want to reset everything. You can restore the camera to its original default settings by going to the Set-up 3 menu ✌ and selecting [Clear settings], then pressing ⑳. You can clear all camera settings, copyright data (see page xxx), or just the Custom Function settings.

Viewfinder

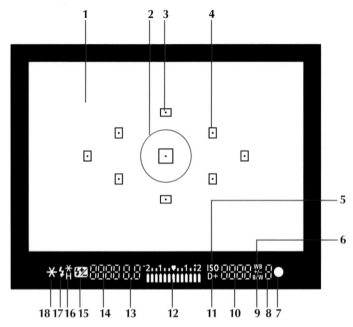

1. Focusing Screen
2. Spot metering screen
3. **AF** point display indicator
4. **AF** points
5. ISO speed
6. White balance correction WB
7. Focus confirmation light ●
8. Max. burst
9. Monochrome shooting **B/W**
10. Exposure level indicator
    Exposure compensation amount
    AEB range
11. **D+** High tone priority
12. Exposure level indicator
    Exposure compensation amount
    AEB range

Red-eye reduction lamp-on indicator
13. Aperture
14. Card full warning **FuLL**
    Card error warning **Err**
    No card warning **Card**
    Shutter speed
    FE lock **FEL**
    Busy **buSY**
    Built-in flash recycling
    (**⁵ buSY**)
15. Flash Exposure Compensation 🔲
16. **⁵ʜ** High-speed sync (FP flash)
    ⁵* FE lock /
    FEB in-progress
17. **⁵** Flash-ready / Improper FE lock warning
18. **✳** AE lock /
    AEB in-progress

36

The Viewfinder

The Rebel T1i uses a standard eye-level, reflex viewfinder with a fixed pentamirror. Images from the lens are reflected to the viewfinder by a quick return, semi-transparent half-mirror (there is no cutoff with Canon lenses EF 600mm f/4L IS USM or shorter). The mirror lifts for the exposure, then rapidly returns to keep viewing blackout to a very short period. Viewfinder blackout time is about 130 milliseconds at shutter speeds of 1/60 second or faster. The mirror is also dampened so that its bounce and vibration are essentially eliminated. The viewfinder shows approximately 95% of the actual image area captured by the sensor. The eyepoint is about 19 millimeters, which is good for people with glasses. (The higher the eyepoint number, the farther your eye can be from the viewfinder and still see the whole image.)

The viewfinder features a non-interchangeable, precision matte focusing screen. It uses special micro-lenses to make manual focusing easier and to increase viewfinder brightness. The viewfinder provides 0.87x magnification and includes superimposition display optics to make information easy to see in all conditions. The display includes a great deal of data about camera settings and functions, though not all these numbers are available at once. The camera's nine autofocus (AF) points are superimposed on the focusing screen, and the solid band at the bottom of the screen shows most of the shooting information that you need.

Depth of field can be previewed through the viewfinder using the Depth-of-field preview button, located near the lens on the lower-left front of the camera. When you first press the depth-of-field button, all you may notice is that the viewfinder darkens in relation to the aperture setting. Don't be concerned about that; this is just a tool to examine focus. With practice you'll learn to concentrate on the fine details of objects in the scene to see if they are in focus.

There is no eyepiece shutter to block light entering the viewfinder when it is not against the eye (which affects exposure metering). However, an eyepiece cover, conveniently stored on the camera strap, is provided instead. It is necessary to remove the eyecup to attach the eyepiece cap.

Viewfinder Adjustment

The viewfinder adjustment diopter can bring the focusing screen into sharp view.

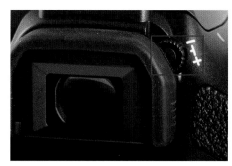

The Rebel T1i's viewfinder features a built-in diopter (a supplementary lens that allows for sharper viewing). The diopter helps you get a sharp view of the focusing screen so you can be sure you are getting the correct focus as you shoot. For this to work properly, you need to adjust the diopter for your eye. The adjustment knob is just above the eyecup, slightly to the right. Fine-tune the diopter setting by looking through the viewfinder at the AF points. Then rotate the dioptric adjustment knob until the AF points appear sharp. You should not look at the subject that the camera is focused on, but at the actual focal points on the viewfinder screen. If you prefer, you can also use the information at the bottom of the screen for this purpose.

While some people can use this adjustment to see through the camera comfortably with or without eyeglasses, I have found that the correction isn't really strong enough for most who wear glasses regularly (like me).

All those pixels in the T1i will produce a great image but only if you make sure your subject is in focus. If the viewfinder diopter isn't set for your vision, getting the subject in focus will be next to impossible.

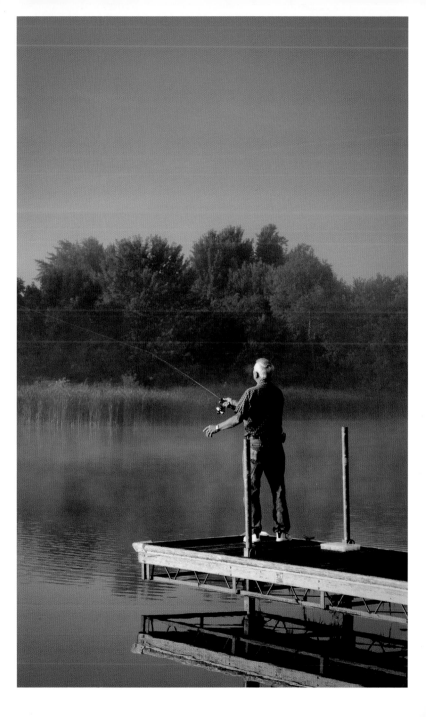

The LCD Monitor

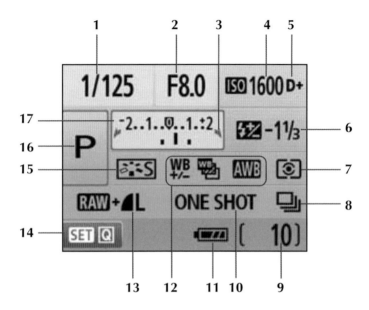

1. Shutter speed
2. Aperture
3. Main Dial pointer
4. ISO speed
5. Highlight tone priority
6. Flash exposure
7. Metering mode
8. Drive mode
9. Shots remaining
10. AF mode
11. Battery check
12. White Balance
13. Image-recording quality
14. Quick control icon
15. Picture style
16. Shooting mode
17. Exposure level indicator

The LCD Monitor

The LCD monitor is probably the one digital camera feature that has most changed how we photograph. Recognizing its importance, Canon has put a 3-inch (7.62 cm—quite large for digital cameras), high-resolution LCD screen in the monitor found on the back of the camera. With about 920,000 pixels, this screen has excellent sharpness, making it extremely useful for evaluating images. The LCD is coated with a new fluorine coat to reduce smudges, three anti-reflective coatings and an extremely durable scratch-resist-ant coating.

LCD Brightness

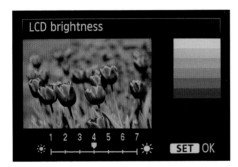

LCD brightness adjusts the LCD screen for better view-ing options in various lighting conditions.

You can adjust the brightness of the LCD monitor to one of seven levels. Press **MENU** and advance to highlight the tab for the Set-up 2 menu **Ý** (color coded yellow) using ⏛. Then use ▲▼ to select [LCD brightness]—the first menu option—and press ⊛. Three things appear on the LCD: the last image captured, a grayscale chart, and a sliding scale that you can adjust with ◀▶. Once you have selected the brightness setting you want, press ⊛ to confirm it and exit the menu screen.

Histogram

The histogram charts the exposure of an image for a more exact exposure evaluation.

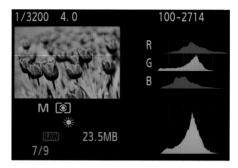

The LCD monitor in the Rebel T1i can also display a graphic representation of exposure values; this graph is called a histogram. The ability to see both the recorded picture and an exposure evaluation graph means that under and overexposures, color challenges, lighting problems, and compositional issues can be dealt with on the spot. Flash photography in particular can be checked, not only for correct exposure, but also for other factors, such as the effect of lighting ratios when multiple flash units and/or reflectors are used. No Polaroid film test is needed. Instead, you can see the actual image captured by the sensor.

Auto Rotate

Auto rotate allows you to view vertical images in the LCD without physically rotating the camera body.

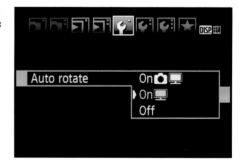

In addition, the camera can rotate images in the LCD monitor. Some photographers love this feature, others hate it, but you have the choice. The Auto rotate function displays vertical images properly without holding the camera in the vertical position—but at a price: The image appears smaller on the LCD. On the other hand, you can keep the image as big as possible by not applying this function, but a vertical picture will appear sideways in the LCD.

Image Magnification

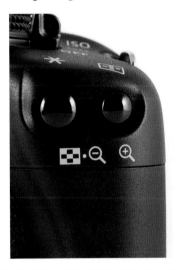

The image magnify and reduce buttons are labeled in blue to signify that these buttons function during playback.

You can also magnify an image up to 10x in the monitor by repeatedly pressing $\oplus$ when in image playback mode. The enlarged photo is scrollable using the four cross keys $\diamond$ so you can inspect all of it. It is a good practice to check focus using this method.

Note: Magnification is only possible during image playback, not image review. Image review happens right after you take the picture. You can jump to playback from review by pressing $\boxdot$ while the image is displayed.

While the image is magnified, you can use $\stackrel{\text{}}{\approx}$ to scroll back and forth through your other images. This way you can compare details in images without having to re-zoom on each one. Use $\boxtimes\cdot\oplus$ to reduce magnification of the image. While you can repeatedly press $\boxtimes\cdot\oplus$ to get back to normal display, the quickest way is to press $\boxdot$. If you press $\boxtimes\cdot\oplus$ when the image isn't magnified, it brings up an image display of 4 images with the first press, or 9 images with the second one. This allows you to jump quickly through your images 4 or 9 images at a time.

Shooting Information

When the LCD monitor is not being used for image review, you can view the current camera settings.

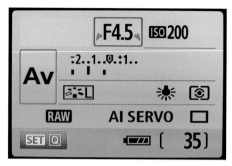

The LCD is not just for displaying images. It is also designed to display shooting information and is always operational when the camera is on. When not used to change menu settings or to play back an image, the LCD displays the current camera settings: exposure, white balance, drive settings, metering type, focusing type, resolution, and much more.

The display-off sensor senses when you are looking through the viewfinder and turns off the LCD monitor automatically.

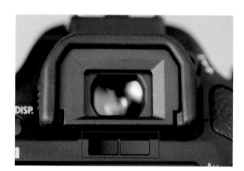

Display-Off Sensor

Although the LCD is always available when the camera is on, a display-off sensor below the viewfinder turns off the display when you bring the camera up to your eye for shooting. This saves power and minimizes distraction when you look through the viewfinder. The sensor works by emitting infrared light that is reflected back to an infrared sensor by any object that passes close to the viewfinder. To save power, you can also turn off the display manually by using the Display button DISP., located on back of the camera to the left of the viewfinder.

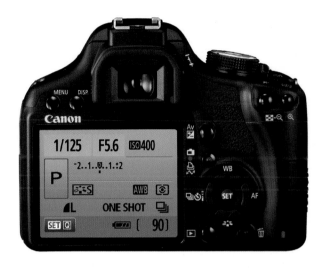

While the shooting information on the LCD is a useful, with the T1i, it also becomes a powerful camera adjustment tool: the Quick Control Screen.

Quick Control Screen

As mentioned above, when it is not in menu mode or play-ing back an image, the T1i displays the shooting settings on the LCD monitor. This display expands on the information that is shown in the viewfinder. It also provides quick access to many of the camera's settings. By pushing straight down on ⊛ you can turn this display into an interactive camera-setting menu called the Quick Control screen.

Once the Quick Control screen is displayed, use ✧ to highlight each of the displayed shooting parameters. When a parameter is highlighted, use 🖾 to change the value that appears on the LCD monitor.

This new Quick Control screen offers quick access to some settings that would normally require multiple button presses to change. For example, to set auto exposure bracketing, normally you would need to first press **MENU**, then use 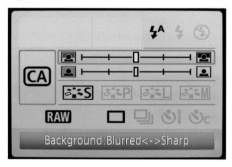 to select ◻, use ▲▼ to select [Expo. comp./AEB], press ⊛ to enter the submenu and then use 📷 to set the bracketing range, and, finally, press ⊛ to accept the setting. Setting image recording quality would require similar steps. When you use the Quick Control screen, not only do you merely highlight the parameter and use 📷 to change the value, it is not necessary to press ⊛ to accept the setting. Just tap the shutter release button to exit and the setting is accepted.

If you want a little more guidance when using the Quick Control screen, press ⊛ when the parameter is highlighted to call up the normal menu options for that parameter (if there is one). For example, you might use the ⊛ button if you want to see a list of all the possible ISO speeds, or if you don't remember which control to use to adjust the auto-exposure bracketing range.

The Quick Control Screen operates differently depending on the shooting mode the T1i is set for. In Creative Auto mode the Quick Control Screen is the only place where you can adjust the unique Background and Exposure adjustments.

Note: In Basic shooting modes, you can only use the Quick Control screen to choose image recording quality and to select Single shooting ◻ drive mode, Self-timer/Remote control ⓣ, or Self-timer:Continuous ⓣc. When in Creative Auto mode ⓒⒶ, you also have access to Continuous shooting ⌷, a limited selection of Picture Styles, flash mode control (Auto flash ⚡ᴬ, Flash on ⚡, and Flash off ⊘), and special background and exposure adjustments.

As previously mentioned, press DISP. to toggle the shooting settings display on and off. But there is another function of DISP.. When any of the main menu tabs is displayed (not when a submenu is displayed) press DISP. to bring up the camera settings display. This information includes:

- Remaining capacity on the memory card in megabytes (MB) or gigabytes (GB).
- Current color space
- Current white balance shift and bracketing setting
- Live View shooting enabled status
- Auto sensor cleaning status
- Auto power off timer setting
- Beeper on/off status
- Red-eye reduction enabled status
- Auto rotate setting
- LCD monitor auto off status
- Date and Time

Press DISP. again to go back to the menu or tap the shutter release button to go quickly back to shooting mode.

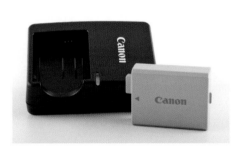

It is best to charge the battery just before shooting. All recharge-able batteries lose a little of their charge every day. If you are shooting a lot, extra batteries are a must. Canon brand batteries are worth the money.

T1i Batteries

Canon has included a high performance battery for the T1i. At 1080mAh in capacity, the lithium ion LP-E5 battery is a great improvement over previous digital Rebel batteries. Milliamp Hours (mAh) indicate a battery's capacity to hold a charge. Higher mAh numbers mean longer-lasting batteries.

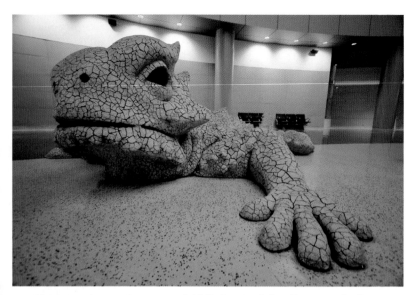

You never know where you might find a good shooting opportunity—even airports can present chances for an interesting photo. Always pack a back-up battery in your camera bag, just in case.

Although the camera is designed for efficient use of battery power, it is important to understand that power consumption is highly dependent on how long certain features are active. The more the camera features are utilized, the shorter the battery life, especially with regard to use of the LCD, built-in flash, Live View, and video recording. Be sure to have backup batteries, and shut the camera off if you are not using it.

Canon estimates that at 73°F (23°C), the battery will last approximately 500 shots when flash is not used, or 400 shots when flash is used 50% of the time. Lower temperatures reduce the number of shots. In addition, it is never wise to expose your camera or its accessories to heat or direct sunlight (i.e., don't leave the camera sitting in your car on a hot or a cold day!). When you use the Live View feature, the number of shots drops to 190, or 170 with 50%

flash usage. The approximate length of time you can shoot continuously with Live View is 1 hour at 73°F (23°C) with a fully charged battery. The LP-E5 is rated at 7.4 volts and it takes about 2 hours to fully charge on the LC-E5 charger that is included with the camera.

The Battery Grip BG-E5 attaches to the bottom of the camera and can be used with one or two LP-E5 batteries. If two batteries are loaded, power is initially drawn from the battery having the higher voltage. Once the voltage level of the two batteries is the same, power is drawn from both packs. When used, the BG-E5 replaces the internal battery of the T1i. The grip also has an adapter, BGM-E5A, which allows six AA-size batteries to be used.

Note: There are a few limitations if you use AA batteries with the grip. The T1i will not let you peform a manual cleaning of the image sensor. The battery indicator may show that there is no (or little) power left in the batteries

A nice feature of the battery grip is that the camera feels the same whether you shoot vertically or horizontally. The battery grip duplicates several controls on the camera so that they are just as easy to access as their horizontal counterparts. The duplicate controls include a shutter button, AE lock button ✱, power switch, Main dial 🕮, exposure compensation button AV☒, and AF point selection button ⊞/🔍.

The AC Adapter Kit (ACK-E5) is useful to those who need the camera to remain consistently powered up (e.g., for scientific lab work, in-studio use, and lengthy video shooting). You can charge the battery in the car using the CBC-E5 12V charger.

Date/Time

Date and time are established by going to the Set-up 2 menu ⚡. Next use ▲▼ to select [Date/Time]. Press ⑯ to enter the adjustment mode. Once there, use ◄► to step through each parameter on the screen. When you are on a setting, press ⑯ to enter the adjustment mode and use ▲▼ to adjust the value. Press ⑯ again to accept the setting. Continue using the cross keys and ⑯ to adjust the date, time and/or to format the date/time display. Once the date and time are correct, use the cross keys to highlight [OK] and press ⑯ again to confirm your selections and exit the adjustment mode.

A special rechargeable battery inside the battery compartment holds the date and time in memory even when you remove the LP-E5 battery. This special battery gets its recharge power from the LP-E5. Normally you don't need to worry about this, but if you store the T1i for long periods of time without an LP-E5 installed, the camera may lose date and time. All you have to do is to install an LP-E5 and the date time battery will recharge.

The Sensor

The Rebel T1i has a newly designed 15.1 MP sensor (4752 x 3168 pixels), which is remarkable in a camera of this class, especially given the Rebel T1i's price and speed. It can easily be used for quality magazine reproduction across a two-page spread.

Because the Rebel T1i's APS-sized CMOS sensor (22.3 x 14.9 mm; APS stands for Advanced Photo System and describes a small-format sensor) covers a smaller area than a 35mm film frame, it records a narrower field of view than a 35mm film camera. To help photographers who are used to working with 35mm SLRs visualize this narrower field of view, a cropping factor of 1.6 is applied to the lens focal length number. Thus, on the Rebel T1i, a 200mm lens has a field of view similar to that of a 320mm lens on a 35mm camera. Remember, the focal length of the lens doesn't change, just the view seen by the Rebel T1i's sensor.

This focal length conversion factor is great for telephoto advocates because a 400mm telephoto acts like a 640mm lens on a 35mm camera. However, at the wide-angle end a lens loses most of its wide-angle capabilities — a 28mm lens acts like a 45mm lens. The Rebel T1i accepts not just Canon EF lenses, but also Canon EF-S lenses (see page 204), which are specially designed for this size image sensor. You can use the Canon 10-22mm zoom if you want to shoot wide-angle pictures; it offers an equivalent 16-35mm focal length.

Though small-format, the sensor in the Rebel T1i demonstrates improvements in sensor technology. It adds more pixels than the Rebel XSi, on the same size image sensor. Obviously, then, each pixel has to be smaller. In the past, this would have meant problems with noise, sensitivity, dynamic range, and reduced continuous shooting speed. However, this sensor's 15.1 MPs offer great signal-to-noise performance, dynamic range, and ISO speed range. And despite the larger number of pixels, the continuous shooting speed for JPEG images has also increased.

Low noise characteristics are extremely important to advanced amateur and professional photographers who want the highest possible image quality. The Rebel T1i gives an extraordinarily clean image with exceptional tonalities and it can be enlarged with superior results.

Several other factors contribute to the improved imaging quality. Canon has worked hard on the design and production of its sensors. (They are one of the few digital SLR manufacturers that make their own sensors.) The microlens configuration has been improved to increase light-gathering ability, improve light convergence, and reduce light loss. The area that is sensitive to light on each pixel has also been increased.

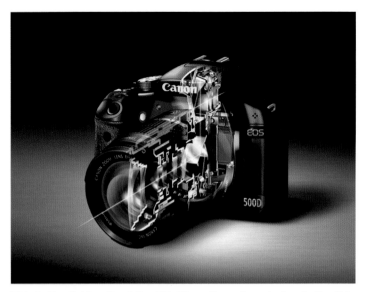

This is the light path of the T1i. The reflex mirror (reflex is the R in SLR) bounces light from the lens into the viewfinder prism. The prism send the light out to the viewfinder eye piece and also to the autofocus sensors.

In addition, the camera has an improved low-noise, high-speed output amplifier as well as power-saving circuitry that also reduces noise. With such low noise, the sensor offers more range and flexibility in sensitivity settings. ISO settings range from 100-3200 (expandable to 12,800).

The on-chip RGB primary color filter uses a standard Bayer pattern over the sensor elements. This is an alternating arrangement of color with 50% green, 25% red, and 25% blue; full color is interpolated from the data. In addition, an infrared cut-off, low-pass filter is located in front of the sensor. This two-part filter is designed to prevent the false colors and the wavy or rippled look of surfaces (moiré) that can occur when photographing small, patterned areas with high-resolution digital cameras.

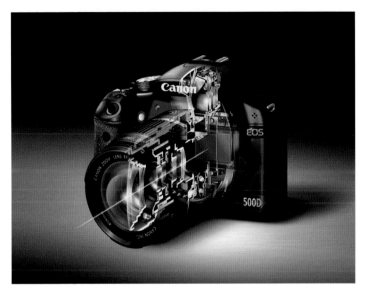

This is also what happens when the camera is in Live Video and recording movies.

Mirror Lockup

For really critical work on a tripod, such as shooting long exposures or working with macro and super telephoto lenses, sharpness is improved by eliminating the vibrations caused by mirror movement. This is accomplished by locking up the mirror in advance using the Rebel T1i's mirror lockup function. However, it also means the viewfinder is blacked out and the drive mode is Single shooting ☐.

   Mirror lockup is set with Custom Function 9 (C.Fn-9, see page 78). Once set, the mirror locks up when the shutter button is pressed. Press the shutter button again to make the exposure. The mirror flips back down if you don't press the shutter within 30 seconds.

Use a remote switch or the self-timer to keep all movement to a minimum. With the self-timer, the shutter goes off 2 seconds after the mirror is locked up, allowing vibrations to dampen. When you use the self-timer with Bulb exposure (see page 148) and mirror lockup, you must keep the shutter depressed during the two-second self-timer countdown, otherwise you will hear a shutter sound but the image will not be captured.

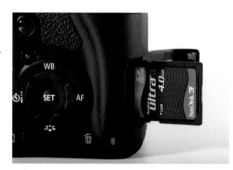

Large memory cards are a necessity. Make sure that you travel with a couple. Look for the SDHC logo when buying SD cards. If your are recording HD video make sure the speed class of the card is 6 or greater.

Memory Cards

The Canon EOS Rebel T1i uses Secure Digital (SD) memory cards. You need a sizeable card to handle the image files of this camera; anything less than 512 MB fills up too quickly (see page 113 for specifics). SD cards are sturdy, durable, and difficult to damage. One thing they don't like is heat; make sure you store them properly.

There are two different kinds of SD cards: SD and SD high capacity (SDHC). The T1i supports both cards, but it is important to know the difference when you start downloading your images to the computer. An SDHC card fits into an SD slot, and other than the distinction in logos, is impossible to visually distinguish from an SD card. (The regular SD card was developed first; SDHC came later, offering larger capacities.)

The capacity difference between SD and SDHC doesn't affect the Rebel T1i. However, SDHC cards cannot be used on older SD devices, such as card readers or printers. If you deliver an SDHC card directly to someone for printing rather than printing your images yourself, make sure they can use an SDHC memory card. Likewise, if you have older SD devices, they might not support SDHC.

SDHC-capable slots, including the one in the Rebel T1i, have no problem using regular SD cards. This simple rule applies: SDHC-capable devices can use either SD or SDHC cards and SD devices can only use SD cards. Remember to look for the SDHC label on all your devices if you plan to use SDHC. If this is your first camera and card reader, I would just stick to SDHC cards.

Note: Be wary of SD cards that are greater than 2GB but that don't have the SDHC icon. They may not be reliable. When you try to use an SD reader to read your memory card, your computer may be unable to read the data.

Besides a capacity rating, SDHC cards also have a speed class that specifies how quickly the card can read and write data. If you are shooting video with your T1i you'll need to make sure that the memory card you are using has a speed class of 6.

To remove the memory card from your camera, simply open the card slot cover on the right side of the body. Press gently on the edge of the memory card to release it from the camera. Carefully grab the edge of the card to remove it.

Caution: Before removing the memory card, it is a good idea to turn the camera off. Even though the Rebel T1i automatically shuts itself off when the memory card door is opened, make sure the access lamp on the back of the camera near the bottom right is not illuminated or flashing. This habit of turning the camera off allows the camera to finish writing to the card. If you should open the card slot and remove the card before the camera has written a set of files to it, there is a good possibility you will corrupt the directory or damage the card. You may lose not only the image being recorded, but also potentially all of the images on the card.

Warning: Don't take pictures with very low battery power. If you should lose power while the camera is writing to the card, the entire card could become corrupted, making it nearly impossible to read any files on the memory card.

You have three choices in how the camera numbers the images on the card. They can go continuously from 0001 to 9999, even when you change cards [Continuous]. Or, the camera can reset numbers every time you change cards [Auto reset]. Lastly, you can manually reset the numbering [Manual reset].

The Continuous file numbering option stores all of the images in one folder on the card. Once image 9999 is recorded, the camera tells you that you need to replace the card. At that point you have to replace the SD card or change the numbering options.

Note: Even if you delete images, the maximum number for an image is 9999.

When you use the Auto reset option, numbering is reset to 0001 and a new folder is created each time the memory card is inserted into the camera. The Manual reset option allows you to immediately create a new folder and reset the file numbering to 0001 without having to remove and re-insert the memory card. The maximum number of folders is 999. At 999, you get a "Folder number full" message on the LCD.

There is no advantage to a particular method of numbering; it is a personal preference depending on how you want to manage your images. Continuous numbers can make it easy to track image files over a specific time period. Creating folders and resetting numbers lets you organize a shoot by location or subject matter. To select Continuous, Auto reset, or Manual reset, go to ♥ and select [File numbering].

Formatting Your Memory Card

Before you use a memory card in your camera, it must be formatted specifically for the Rebel T1i. To do so, go to ❤️ and use ▲▼ to highlight [Format]. Press ⑤ and the Format menu appears on the LCD. It tells you how much of the card is presently filled with images and how big the card is. Use ✣ to select [OK], press ⑤, and formatting begins. You will see a screen showing the progress.

Caution: Formatting your memory card erases all images and information that has been stored there, including protected images. Be sure that you do not need to save anything on the card before you format. (Transfer important images to a computer or another downloading device before formatting the card.)

The format screen also gives the option of performing a low level format of the card. Low level formatting rebuilds the card's file structure and flags any memory locations that are unreliable. While low level formatting takes more time, it is a good idea to do this on a relatively frequent basis—I do it every time. Press the Erase button 🗑, located on the back of the camera in the lower right corner, and put a check mark in the Low level format box.

It is important to routinely format a memory card to keep its data structure organized. However, never format the card in a computer. A computer uses different file structures than a digital camera and may cause problems. For trouble-free operation always format your card rather than erasing all the images.

Note: My experience is that if memory cards are going to fail, they usually fail at first use. Always test a new card by formatting it, taking pictures and/or recording video, and then downloading the images and video to a computer. Resist the temptation to buy a new card and put it directly into your camera bag at the start of a long trip; open it up and test it to make sure it works.

Cleaning the Camera

A clean camera minimizes the amount of dirt or dust that could reach the sensor. A good kit of cleaning materials should include the following: A soft camel hair brush to clean off the camera, an antistatic brush and micro-fiber cloth for cleaning the lens, a pack towel for drying the camera in damp conditions (available at outdoor stores), and a small rubber bulb to blow debris off the lens and the camera.

Always blow and brush debris from the camera before rubbing with any cloth. For lens cleaning, blow and brush first, then clean with a micro-fiber cloth. If you find there is residue on the lens that is hard to remove, you can use lens-cleaning fluid, but ensure it is made specifically for camera lenses. Never apply the fluid directly to the lens, as it can seep behind the lens elements and get inside the body of the lens. Apply with a cotton swab, or just spray the edge of a micro-fiber cloth. Rub gently to remove the dirt, and then buff the lens with a dry part of the cloth, which you can wash in the washing machine when it gets dirty.

You don't need to be obsessive, but remember that a clean camera and lens help ensure that you don't develop image problems. Dirt and residue on the camera can get inside when changing lenses. If these end up on the sensor, you will have image problems. Dust on the sensor appears as small, dark, out-of-focus spots in the photo (most noticeable in light areas, such as sky). You can minimize problems with sensor dust if you turn the camera off when changing lenses (preventing a dust-attracting static charge from building up). Keep a body cap on the camera and lens caps on lenses when not in use. You should regularly vacuum your camera bag so that dust and dirt aren't stored with the camera.

The T1i has a built-in system to combat the dust that is inherent with cameras that use removable lenses. This system uses a two-pronged approach: (1) The camera self-cleans to remove dust from the sensor, and (2) it employs a dust detection system to remove dust artifacts from images using software on your computer.

The low-pass filter in front of the sensor is attached to a piezoelectric element that rapidly vibrates at camera power-up and power-down. While self-cleaning at power up just before taking pictures seems like an obvious time to clean the sensor, why clean it at power down? Cleaning at power-down prevents dust from sticking to the sensor when the camera sits for long periods of time.

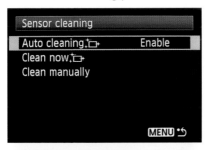

Self-cleaning can be enabled and disabled under Set-up 2 menu ♥⁼. Use ▲▼ to highlight [Sensor cleaning] and press ⑤. In the Sensor cleaning submenu, select [Auto cleaning] 🗁 and press ⑤. From there you can choose to enable or disable self-cleaning, then press ⑤ to accept your selection. You can also engage the self-cleaning function immediately or start the manual sensor cleaning procedure (see page 60).

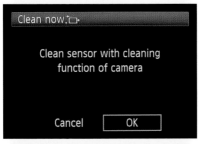

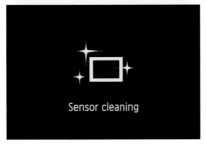

Note: In order to prevent overheating, the self-cleaning operation cannot be engaged within 3 seconds of any other operation. It also stops working if it is run 5 times within 10 seconds. After a brief delay (usually 10 seconds) it will be available for use.

In the event that there is still dust on the sensor, the Rebel T1i's Dust Delete Data feature can be used. By photographing an out-of-focus, pattern-less, solid white object (such as a white sheet of paper), the image sensor is able to detect the shadow cast by dust stuck to the low-pass filter. Coordinates of the dust are embedded in the image metadata. Canon's Digital Photo Professional version 3.6 (supplied with the T1i) can use this data to automatically remove the dust spots in the image.

Note: The Dust Delete data can only be used by Canon software.

Manually Cleaning the Sensor

The Rebel T1i allows you to clean the sensor, but there are precautions to be taken. You must do this carefully and gently, indoors and out of the wind—and at your own risk! Your battery must be fully charged so it doesn't fail during cleaning (or you can use the optional AC adapter). The sensor unit is a precision optical device, so if the gentle cleaning described below doesn't work, you should send the camera to a Canon Service Center for a thorough cleaning.

To clean the sensor, turn the camera on and go to ♥⁺. Using ▲▼, highlight [Sensor cleaning] and press ⊛. Use ▲▼ in the Sensor cleaning submenu to highlight [Clean manually] and press ⊛, then follow the instructions. You'll see options for [OK] and [Cancel]. Using ◄►, select [OK] and press ⊛. The LCD turns off, the mirror locks up, and the shutter opens. Take the lens off. Holding the camera face down, use a blower to gently blow any dust or other debris off the bottom of the lens opening first, and then blow off the sensor. Do not use brushes or compressed air because these can damage the sensor's surface. Turn the camera off

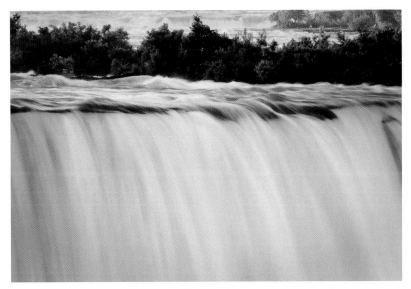

Images with large areas of white, such as the one shown here, can reveal spots caused by a dusty sensor.

when done. The mirror and shutter will return to normal. Put the lens back on.

Caution: Canon specifically recommends against any cleaning techniques or devices that touch the surface of the imaging sensor. If manual cleaning doesn't work, contact a Canon Service Center for cleaning.

Never leave a D-SLR without a body cap for any length of time. Lenses should be capped when not in use and rear caps should always be used when a lens is not mounted. Also, make sure you turn off the camera when you change lenses. These practices help to prevent dust from reaching the sensor.

Getting Started in 10 Basic Steps

There are ten things you should check in order to make your work with the camera easier from the start. These steps are especially useful if you have not yet become familiar with the camera. You will probably modify them with experience.

1. Adjust the eyepiece: Use the dioptric adjustment knob to the right of the viewfinder to make the focus through your eyepiece as sharp as possible. You can adjust it with a fingertip. (See page 38.)

2. Set [Auto power off] for a reasonable time: The default duration in the ♈ is merely 30 seconds. I guarantee this will frustrate you when the camera has turned itself off just as you are ready to shoot. Perhaps it is more realistic to try [4 min.]. (See page 34.)

3. Choose a large file size (L for JPEG, or RAW): This determines your image recording quality. Select ◻, then press ⊛ and use ◄► to select your desired image size (see page 113). You are usually best served by choosing one of the high-quality options.

4. Set your preferred shooting mode: Use the Mode dial ◉ on the top right shoulder of the camera to select any of the Basic Zones (see pages 137-140) or Creative Zones (see pages 140-148). If using any of the Creative Zones, select a Picture Style. (See page 93.)

5. Choose AF mode: Autofocus (AF) mode is set by pressing the ►AF key when a menu isn't displayed on the LCD. The LCD monitor then displays several AF mode options. The selected mode displays in the camera settings on the LCD. A good place to start on this camera is AI Servo AF. (See page 120.)

6. Select a drive mode: Drive mode is selected by pressing the ◄⌸/◷ button when a menu isn't displayed on the LCD. Select either Single shooting ◻, Continuous shooting

,, Self-timer/Remote control ⟳i, Self-timer:2 sec ⟳₂, or Self-timer:Continuous ⟳c. (See page 124.) The LCD indicates the mode the camera is in. Depending on the shooting mode, not all options will be available.

7. Choose metering mode: Metering mode is set via ▣. Use ▲▼ to highlight [Metering mode] and press ⊛. Choose from four different metering modes: ◙ – Evaluative, ◙ – Partial, ⊡ – Spot, or ▢ – Center-weighted average. Evaluative ◙ is a good starting point. (See page 129.)

8. Select white balance (WB): Auto white balance ᴀᴡʙ is a good default white balance setting because the Rebel T1i is designed to generally do well with it. To set, press the ▲WB button. (See pages 101-109.) The different white balance choices display on the monitor. After making your choice, the selected white balance appears in the camera settings display on the LCD.

9. Pick an ISO setting: Though any setting between ISO 100 and ISO 400 works extremely well, you can generally set higher ISO sensitivity with the Rebel T1i than with other digital cameras and still capture an image with less noticeable noise. (See pages 125.) Press the ISO button located immediately behind ⌂. The LCD monitor displays a range of ISO speed to choose from. Use ⌂ or ◄► to select. You can even change ISO without having to take your eyes away from the viewfinder. When you press the ISO button the information display in the bottom of the viewfinder shows the current ISO setting. Use ⌂ to rotate through the ISO choices.

10. Set a reasonable review time: The default review time on the LCD monitor is only two seconds. That's very little time to analyze your photos, so I recommend the eight-second setting, which you can always cancel by pressing the shutter button. If you are worried about using too much battery power, just turn off the review function altogether. (See page 81.)

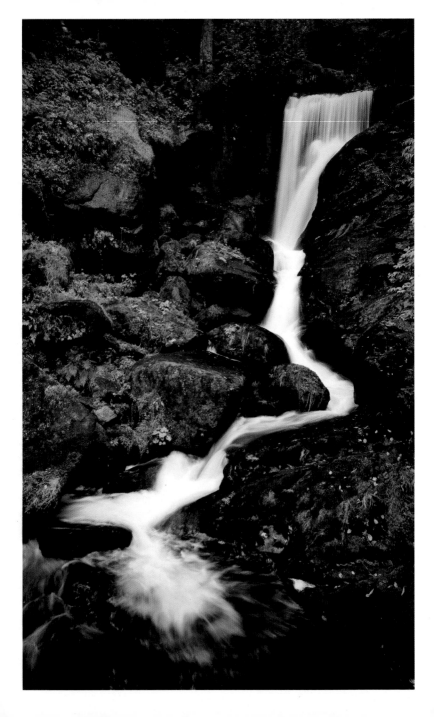

The T1i Menu System and the LCD Monitor

Using the Menus

Menus systems and LCD monitors are two extremely important features that help define digital cameras. In fact, D-SLRs menus are the indispensable way to control the great number of settings found in these sophisticated cameras. Still, in some cameras, menus are a necessary evil because they are not always easy to use. Canon has put a great deal of thought into the design of the Rebel T1i's menus so that they can be used efficiently.

All menu controls, or items, are found in eight menus, grouped into four categories based on their use. These categories, intuitively named in order of appearance within the menu system, are Shooting ◘˙, Playback ⊡˙, Set-up Ƴ˙, and My Menu ☆. You gain access to the Rebel T1i's menu selections whenever you push the Menu button MENU, located on the back of the camera above the top left corner of the LCD monitor. Once the menus are displayed, you can shift from category to category in one of two ways: use the Main dial ⌂, located on the top of the camera just behind the shutter button, or use the left/right cross keys ◄►.

↻ *The Rebel T1i offers many options for shooting, viewing, and processing your images. Familiarizing yourself with the menu system will give you more control over how the camera operates.*

The menus are designated by their icon tab at the top of the menu screen on the LCD monitor. In general, press MENU to display these different tabs. Scroll to highlight your desired menu by using ◄► or ⚙, and you will see choices under the menu tab. Use ▲▼ to highlight a menu item and confirm (lock-in) your selection with ⊛. Some items have further options to choose from, which require you to scroll and select in a similar manner, using the cross keys—▲ WB, ▼ ⚹⚹, ◄⧖/⊙, and ► AF—and ⊛. To back out of a menu, press MENU. Understanding the menu system is necessary in order to fully benefit from using the LCD monitor and the Custom Functions.

Note: When the camera is first used, pressing MENU takes you to the Shooting 1 Menu ◘. After that, pressing MENU takes you to the last menu you selected, even if you have just powered on the camera.

Shooting 1 Menu ◘

It might seem like a silly setting but the Release shutter without card (when turned off) will prevent you from thinking you are taking pictures when you aren't. It is the modern day (digital) equivalent of preventing you from taking a picture without any film in the camera.

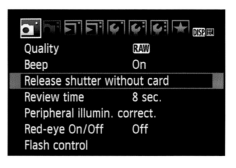

For items that obviously affect actual photography, these two red-coded menus include a number of choices:

[Quality]	Sets image size and resolution, plus selects RAW.
[Beep]	Turns on/off the audible signal for focus and self-timer.
[Release shutter without card]	Allows you to test the camera when no memory card is installed.

[Review time]	Controls how long image stays on LCD monitor after the shot.
[Peripheral illumin. correct.]	Accesses lens vignetting correction sub menu.
[Red-eye On/Off]	Sets red-eye reduction.
[Flash control]*	Sets built-in flash functions, external Speedlite function settings, external Speedlite custom function settings and clears external Speedlite custom functions (Speedlite control is model dependent).

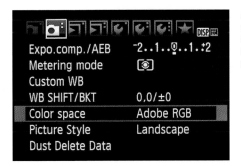

If you use Adobe RGB color space your image file names will start with _MG rather than IMG.

Shooting 2 Menu ◻⋮ *

[Expo.comp./AEB]	Exposure compensation and automatic exposure bracketing.
[Metering mode]	Sets exposure metering method.
[Custom WB]	Manually sets white balance.
[WB SHIFT/BKT]	Used for bracketing and shifting white balance.
[Color space]	sRGB or Adobe RGB.
[Picture Style]	Sets up different profiles for processing images in-camera.
[Dust Delete Data]	Captures reference file for dust extraction.

Playback 1 Menu ⊡

If you haven't set the T1i to embed rotation data in the image files, use this feature to rotate the images to the proper orientation.

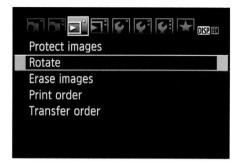

Two blue-coded menus offer several choices for use when viewing images on the LCD monitor.

[Protect images]	Prevents images from being erased.
[Rotate]	Rotates image so vertical pictures display vertically.
[Erase images]	Permanently erases selected (or all) images on memory card.
[Print order]	Specifies images to be printed DPOF.
[Transfer order]	Used to select images for transfer to the computer.

Playback 2 Menu ⊡

The brightness histogram is the easiest to read. Use RGB if you need to know which channel is being under or overexposed. Remember that you can use the 4th display mode to view both histograms.

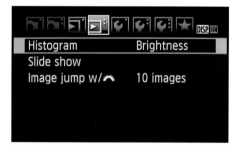

[Histogram]	Selects between Brightness and RGB histograms.
[Slide show]	Automatically creates a "slide show" on LCD monitor; length of image display is user selectable.

68

[Image jump w/🔄]   Sets number of images—1, 10, 100—to jump when using 🔄 to access images during playback. (You can also jump by Date, Movies, or Stills.)

Note: In playback mode, press ▲ WB; this will bring up a little menu of jump choices which you can scroll through using ▲ WB and ▼ 🔄. This is faster than going through Playback 2 menu ▤.

Set-up 1 Menu 🔧

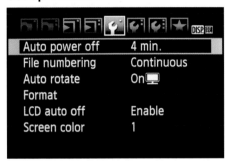

Auto power off	4 min.
File numbering	Continuous
Auto rotate	On
Format	
LCD auto off	Enable
Screen color	1

The default Auto power off setting of 30 seconds can be frustrating, particularly when you are first learning your camera. Try setting it to 4 minutes.

Color coded yellow, the three set-up menus present selections to make before shooting.

[Auto power off]   Seven options for different time periods, as well as no power off.

[File numbering]   Three different options for managing your image file naming.

[Auto rotate]   Determines if a vertical image is rotated in the camera and in the computer; only in the computer; or not rotated.

[Format]   Initializes and/or erases the memory card; very important.

[LCD auto off]   Selects whether or not to turn LCD off when your eye approaches viewfinder.

[Screen color]   Changes the color of the shooting settings display.

Set-up 2 Menu

Sensor cleaning allows access to both manual and automatic sensor cleaning.

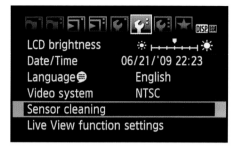

[LCD brightness]   Contains seven levels of viewing brightness.

[Date/Time]   Adjusts date and time that is recorded with images.

[Language]   Options for setting your camera in 25 different languages.

[Video system]   NTSC or PAL.

[Sensor cleaning]   Enables the sensor cleaning function on startup and shutdown; allows you to engage auto clean any time; or permits you to clean the sensor manually.

[Live View function settings]*   Enables Live View; turns on grid for Live View composition; sets meter timer and autofocus mode.

The Set-up 3 menu at first looks simple, but you should think of it really as the doorway to the very dense Custom Function sub menu.

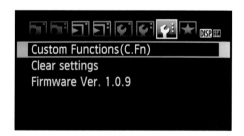

Set-up 3 Menu *

[Custom Functions (C.Fn)]   Allows you to customize camera settings.

[Clear settings]   Returns camera settings to factory-set defaults, clears Custom Functions (C.Fn) and deletes copyright information.

[Firmware Ver.]   Used when updating the camera's software.

My Menu ☆ * (Green)

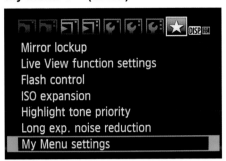

If you want to be fast and efficient when using your T1i, take the time, once you have been using your camera for awhile, to set up this menu. It can be the most useful menu you'll use.

This menu is color coded green:

[My Menu settings]	Provides access to menu items so you can customize a group of frequently used settings for quick access.

Note: The items with an asterisk (*) are not available in the Basic Zone shooting modes, where the camera controls all settings. See pages 137-140..

Note: When Movie mode is selected, a separate Movie menu appears. See Live View and Movie Menus, beginning on page 158.

My Menu ☆

When you first use the Rebel T1i, the My Menu display only has one selection, called [My Menu settings]. Through this selection you can build a custom menu using any of the top-level choices in any of the menus, as well as the custom functions menu tab. My Menu can contain up to six selections.

To build a menu, first press **MENU** and move to the ☆ tab. Highlight [My Menu settings], and then press ⑨. On the [My Menu settings] sub-menu, scroll to highlight [Register] and press ⑨ again. A list of every top-level menu option, including custom functions, is displayed.

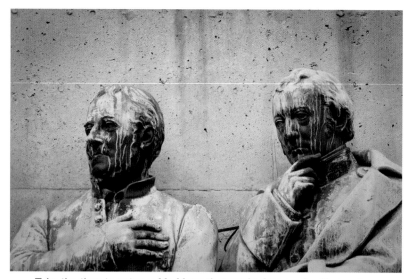
Take the time to setup a My Menu that works for you. It will save time and allows you to concentrate on composition rather than the camera.

Now scroll to select the desired option and press ⊛ again. Highlight [OK] and press ⊛ to confirm the addition of the selected option to ⚷. The option you chose will be grayed out so that you can't insert the same option twice.

Repeat the process until you have selected the options you want, up to a maximum of six. Press the **MENU** button to exit the selection screen, then press **MENU** again to see the resulting My Menu.

The [My Menu settings] sub-menu also allows you to sort your menu items once you've added them to the menu. Select [Sort] from the [My Menu settings] submenu and press ⊛. [Sort My Menu] is displayed, showing the current order of your menu items. Scroll to highlight an item you wish to move. Press ⊛ and an up/down arrow icon appears to the right of the item. Use ▲▼ to move the item up or down in the list. Press ⊛ once the item is in the preferred position and either repeat these steps to change the position of other items, or press **MENU** to exit [Sort My Menu].

If you have filled ⚄ with six items, you must delete an item before you can insert a new one—there is no exchange function. Highlight [Delete] in the [My Menu settings] submenu and press ⑤, then move to highlight an item you wish to delete. Press ⑤ and a confirmation dialog appears. Highlight [OK] and press ⑤. Repeat this process if you wish to delete other My Menu items, then press **MENU** to exit the [Delete My Menu] screen. Similarly you can select [Delete all items] to start with an empty My Menu.

You can customize your Rebel T1i so that ⚄ is displayed every time you press **MENU** (no matter which menu you were last on). To do so, highlight [Display from My Menu] in the [My Menu settings] screen. Press ⑤, highlight [Enable], and press ⑤.

Custom Functions

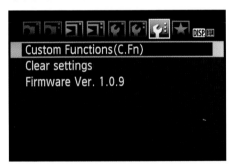

The Custom Functions menu can be a bit overwhelming at first, but with a little practice, it gives you incredible control over your cameras functions.

Like most sophisticated D-SLRs, the Rebel T1i can be customized to fit the unique style and personality of a photographer. Of course, the selection of exposure modes, type of metering, focus choice, drive speed, Picture Style, and so forth, tailor the camera to a specific photographer's needs. However, the Rebel T1i allows for further customization and personalization to help the camera better fit your method and approach to photography. This is done through the Custom Functions (C.Fn) menu. Some photographers never use these settings, while others use them all the time. The camera won't take better photos when you change these settings, but Custom Functions may make the camera easier for you to use.

The Rebel T1i has 13 different built-in Custom Functions, numbered 1-13. They are organized into four groups: C.Fn I–Exposure; C.Fn II–Image; C.Fn III-Auto focus/Drive; and C.Fn IV-Operation/Others.

Custom Functions are found in ♥⁝. Select [Custom Functions (C.Fn)], then press ⑤ to enter the [Custom Functions] screen. Once there, navigate to the desired Custom Function (function numbers are displayed at the bottom of the LCD monitor), and again press ⑤. Highlight the setting you want to use and press ⑤ to accept. To exit the Custom Functions menu, press **MENU** or lightly tap the shutter release button.

Here is a brief summary and commentary on the various Custom Functions. Note that the first selection in each Custom Function is the default setting for the camera.

C.Fn I: Exposure

1 Exposure level increments
This sets the size of incremental steps for shutter speeds, apertures, exposure compensation, and autoexposure bracketing (AEB).

0:	[1/3-stop] The increment is 1/3 stop.
1:	[1/2-stop]

2 ISO expansion
This setting allows you to extend the ISO speed range into the expanded ISO values.

0:	[Off] Normal ISO range of camera, 100-3,200
1:	[On] Expanded ISO range of camera, 100-12,800

Note: ISO 6,400 is represented by "H1"; ISO 12,800 is represented by "H2".

3 Flash sync. speed in Av mode

Sets the flash sync in aperture priority mode either to automatic adjustment or a fixed setting. When set for default
(0:Auto), you can use flash for slow shutter speeds. The slow
shutter speeds can cause blurred elements in your scene.
Option 1 limits the slow shutter speed to no slower than
1/60 so there is less blurring. To lessen blur even more,
option 2 forces the T1i to always use 1/200 when a flash is
engaged.

0:	[Auto]
1:	[1/200-1/60 sec. auto]
2:	[1/200 sec. (fixed)]

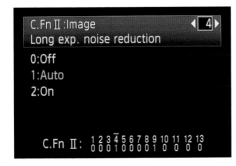

*At the bottom of all
custom function
screens is a quick sta-
tus display showing
how each Custom
Function is currently
set. The top number is
the Function number
the bottom is the cur-
rent setting. If the set-
ting digit is blue that
means it has been
changed from the
default setting.*

C.Fn II: Image

4 Long exp. noise reduction

This setting engages automatic noise reduction for long
exposures. When noise reduction is used, the processing
time of the image is a little more than twice the original
exposure. For example, a 20-second exposure takes an additional 20 seconds to complete.

| 0: | [Off] Long exposure noise reduction is turned off. |
| 1: | [Auto] Noise reduction is turned on if the expo-
sure is 1 second or longer and noise common to
long exposures is detected. |
| 2: | [On] Noise reduction is turned on for all 1 second
or longer exposures even if no noise is detected. |

5 High ISO speed noise reduct'n

As you increase the apparent sensitivity of the T1i by using high ISO settings, you increase the noise in the image. This custom function helps to reduce that noise. When set to [Strong], it decreases the number of shots that can be captured in a row, and white balance bracketing is turned off.

0:        [Standard]
1:        [Low]
2:        [Strong]
3:        [Disable]

If you find yourself constantly accessing a custom function, consider adding it to your My Menu.

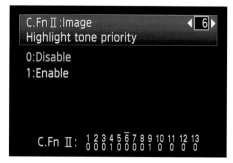

6 Highlight tone priority

This is one of the Rebel T1i's more interesting Custom Functions. Enable this option to expand dynamic range near the bright area of the tone curve. When enabled, the ISO speed range available is 200-3200. You may see more noise in the dark areas of the image when enabled.

0:        [Disable]
1:        [Enable]

Note: When the T1i has highlight tone priority enabled, **D+** will be displayed in the viewfinder and on the LCD monitor.

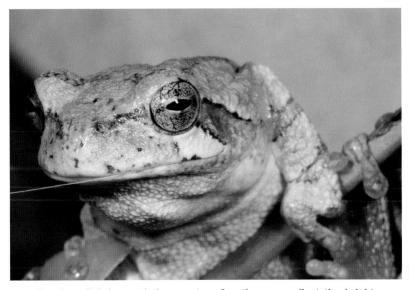

The Auto lighting optimizer custom function can adjust the brightness and contrast of an image without further processing on the computer.

7 Auto Lighting Optimizer

When this function is enabled in difficult exposure situations where the scene is dark, the T1i automatically adjusts the brightness and contrast of the image. In Basic Zone shooting modes, the optimizer is engaged (0:Standard) automatically.

0:     [Standard]
1:     [Low]
2:     [Strong]
3:     [Disable]

Note: When you shoot RAW, you will only see the effect of the Auto Lighting Optimizer if the RAW image is processed via Digital Photo Professional.

C.Fn III: Autofocus/Drive

8 AF-assist beam firing

This controls the AF-assist beam, a series of rapid low-power flash bursts that are useful when operating autofocus in low-light situations.

0:          [Enable] The AF-assist beam is emitted whenever appropriate.

1:          [Disable] This cancels the AF-assist beam.

2:          [Only external flash emits] In low light, an accessory EX flash unit fires its AF-assist beam. The built-in flash's AF-assist feature is disabled.

When shooting with long shutter speeds, use mirror lockup to reduce camera vibration caused by the mirror flipping up.

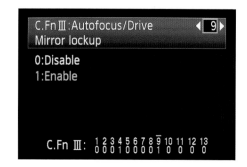

9 Mirror lockup

This Custom Function turns Mirror lockup on or off. Mirror lockup is used to minimize camera shake during exposures.

0:          [Disable] The mirror functions normally.

1:          [Enable] The mirror moves up and locks in position with the first push of the shutter button (press fully). With the second full pressing of the shutter button, the camera takes the picture and the mirror returns to its original position. After 30 seconds, this setting automatically cancels.

C.Fn IV: Auto Operation/Others

10 Shutter/AE lock button

This controls the functions of the shutter and AE lock buttons and can be one of the more confusing custom functions. The best way to read this setting is to pay attention to the slash (/) between Shutter and AE lock button in the description. The shutter button controls the function listed in front of the slash, while the AE lock button ✱ controls the operation listed after it.

0: [AF/AE lock] Autofocus is initiated when the shutter button is depressed halfway / Exposure is locked with ✱.

1: [AE lock/AF] The shutter button locks exposure when depressed halfway / Autofocus is initiated with ✱.

2: [AF/AF lock, no AE lock] The shutter button starts autofocus but when in **AI SERVO** mode you can use ✱ to momentarily stop autofocus in case something passes in front of the camera. Exposure is not locked until the picture is taken.

3: [AE/AF, no AE lock] The shutter button sets exposure but doesn't lock it until the picture is taken / ✱ lets you start and stop autofocus in **AI SERVO**.

11 Assign SET button

This setting assigns new options to ⊛ when shooting.

0: [Quick Control screen] ⊛ allows access to controls on shooting settings display.

1: [Image quality] ⊛ goes directly to recording quality. (This is useful if you want the ability to quickly change from RAW to JPEG.) The settings appear in the LCD monitor.

2: [Flash exposure comp.] ⊛ takes you to the flash exposure compensation screen. (This is useful if you take a lot of flash pictures.)

3: [LCD monitor On/Off] ⊛ acts like the DISP. button (some people find this more convenient).

4: [Menu display] ⊛ acts like the MENU button.

12 LCD display when power ON

This function keeps track of whether the LCD monitor has been turned off to save power.

0:       [Display] LCD displays camera settings when the power switch is turned on.

1:       [Retain power OFF status] When the power switch is turned on, the LCD display stays off if you have used DISP. to turn off the LCD.

13 Add original decision data

This function is used with the Original Data Security Kit OSK-E3, an optional Canon-designed software package. The software is used to authenticate the image data when used in forensic and other specialized applications. When turned on, the captured image is embedded with verification data.

0:       [Off]

1:       [On]

Using Your LCD Monitor

The LCD monitor is one of the most useful tools available when you shoot digital, giving immediate access to your images. You can set your camera so that the image appears for review on the LCD directly after shooting the picture. It's better than a Polaroid print!

The Rebel T1i's 3-inch (7.62 cm) color LCD monitor is much brighter than the monitors of just a couple years ago, but it still takes a little practice to see it well in bright light. You can adjust its brightness level in the Set-up 2 menu ✇ by scrolling to select the option for [LCD brightness]. Confirm by pressing ⊛. However, a bright LCD monitor often makes the image harder to evaluate. The easiest thing to do is to shade the monitor in bright light by using your hand, a hat, or your body to block the sun.

When photographers compare a point-and-shoot digital camera with a larger digital SLR, they often notice that the smaller camera's LCD monitor can be turned on while

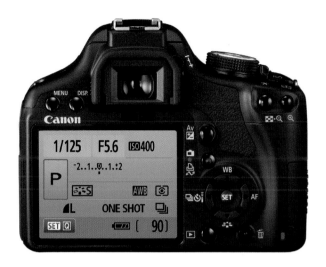

The LCD monitor displays current shooting information when it is not being used for image review.

shooting. Digital point-and-shoot cameras have so-called "live" LCD monitors. Most digital SLRs, however, use a mirror inside the camera (that blocks the path of light from subject to sensor) to direct the image from the lens to the viewfinder. During exposure, the mirror flips up to expose the sensor to light from the image. A live LCD monitor, on the other hand, must be able to see what is coming from the lens at all times in order to feed the LCD monitor. The Rebel T1i has a Live View mode that locks the mirror in the up position and allows you to see what the image sensor sees (see page 157).

LCD Image Review
You can choose to instantly review the image you just shot, and you can also look at all of the previously recorded images stored on your SD card. Most photographers like the immediate feedback of reviewing their images because it allows them to tell if the picture is properly exposed and composed. If not, they can reshoot the scene if that will improve the photo.

It is frustrating to examine a picture and have the instant review function turn off before you are through, so use the T1i's menu system to set the length of time desired to review the images you have just captured. The choices for the duration of review include [2 sec], [4 sec], [8 sec], or [Hold], all controlled by the [Review time] option in ◘˙. You also use this menu selection to activate the [Off] option, which saves power by turning off the LCD monitor, but does not allow you to review the images.

I find that the [2 sec] setting is a bit short; I prefer [8 sec]. You can always turn the review off sooner by lightly pressing the shutter button. The [Hold] setting is good if you like to study your photos, because the reviewed image remains on the LCD monitor until you press the shutter button. But be careful: It is easy to forget to turn off the monitor when you use this selection, in which case your batteries will wear down.

Note: There is a trick that lets you examine the image as long as you like, even when the duration is not set to [Hold]. As the image appears for review, press 🗑 (for erasing) located on the back of the camera near the right corner. This leaves the image on as long as you want (or at least until the Auto power off time is reached). Obviously you have to be careful not to delete the images, so ignore [Erase] and [Cancel] options on the bottom of the screen. Press the shutter button to quit the image review.

Playback

Reviewing images on the LCD monitor is an important benefit of digital cameras. To see not only your most immediate shot, but also any (or all) of the photos stored on the SD card, press the Playback button ▶ on the back of the camera at the bottom right of the LCD monitor. The last image you captured displays on the LCD monitor. You can cycle through the photos by using ◄►. If you start by pressing ◄ ⏱/♻, you move chronologically backward through your images, starting with the most recent one. If you press ► AF, you'll move forward through the images, beginning with the first image on the card.

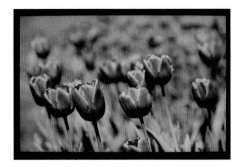

When you press ▶, the image appears on the screen. You can choose the way images are displayed with the DISP. *button.*

Note: Camera buttons with blue-colored labels or icons refer to playback functions.

With the Rebel T1i, you can display the review or playback image in four different formats. Just push DISP., also found on the back of the camera to the left of the viewfinder, and the different views display progressively. By default, image playback appears in the display mode you last used.

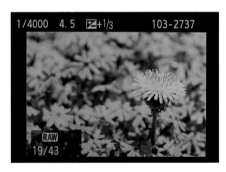

This display modes shows you image as large as it can display on the LCD.

1. Display with basic information: The image for review covers the entire LCD screen and includes superimposed data for folder number, image number, shutter speed, aperture, and exposure compensation.

If you often switch between JPEG and RAW or are concerned about how many images are on the memory card consider using this display option.

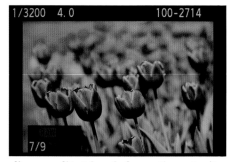

2. Display with recording quality/size information: A display similar to the basic display described above, but image quality/size information is also shown, along with the number of images on the card.

This display includes a histogram, one of the most powerful tools in a digital camera. The histogram will be brightness or RGB depending on the setting in the playback 2 menu.

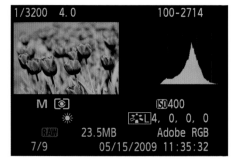

3. Display with full shooting information: A thumbnail of the image is shown with a brightness or RGB histogram and expanded data about how the image was shot (white balance, ISO speed, image recording quality, exposure, and much more). This can be very useful for checking what shooting settings work for you. The thumbnail also includes a Highlight alert function that blinks where areas are overexposed.

4. Display with histogram: The histogram display expands to include both the brightness and RGB histograms. Shooting information is reduced, but includes exposure mode, metering mode, white balance, recording quality, aperture, shutter speed and file size.

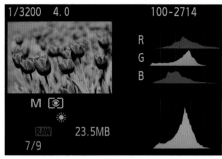

If you want to see both histograms the last display option will show them.

Press the shutter button halfway to stop playback, readying the Rebel T1i to shoot again. You can also stop the playback by pressing ▶.

Freespace	790 MB
Color space	Adobe RGB
WB SHIFT/BKT	0.0/±0
Live View shoot.	Enable
⊡ Enable	◉ Off
ᶻᶻ 4 min.	⬭ On🖵
◖))) On	⌇🗄 Enable
06/21/2009 22:24:44	

This display gives you a quick status report on many of the T1i menu settings. You can only call up this display when you are in one of the T1i menus.

Note: When the camera is in Menu mode (any menu displayed on the LCD monitor), you can press DISP. to show a status display with a whole host of current camera settings. The screen shows color space, white balance shift and bracketing values, Live View shooting setting, auto cleaning of sensor at startup status, red-eye reduction setting, Auto power off timer setting, Auto rotate setting, LCD auto off, and how much space (in MB or GB) is available on the memory card. Press DISP. again to switch back to Menu mode.

Automatic Image Rotation

The Auto rotate setting uses a camera and computer monitor icons to indicate if the T1i will rotate the image on the LCD, and/or embed camera orientation data (horizontal or vertical) in the image file.

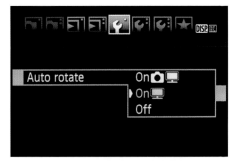

The Rebel T1i includes an option to automatically rotate vertical images during review or playback. To select this function, go to the ♈ menu, highlight [Auto rotate] and press ⑤. You have three options to choose from: **On⚫💻**, **On💻**, and [Off].

   When **On⚫💻** is enabled and the camera is held in a horizontal position, images shot vertically appear up-and-down rather than sideways both in the LCD monitor and when you display them on your computer. You can decide for yourself if you like this option, but I really don't use it much. Sure, the image is upright and you don't have to rotate the camera to view it. But the problem is the size of the image. To get that vertical picture to fit in the horizontal frame of the LCD monitor, it has to be reduced considerably and therefore becomes harder to see. I like to use the second option, **On💻**. This turns off Auto rotate when playing back on the camera, but still lets the computer know that the image should be rotated for display. You must turn on **On⚫💻** or **On💻** before you take a picture so that the rotation data gets embedded in the image file.

Note: When recording video, auto rotation (either on the computer or on the T1i) is not functional. Except in rare situations, it is not a good idea to shoot video with the T1i in a vertical position.

Magnifying the Image

You can make the image larger on the LCD monitor by factors ranging from 1.5x to 10x. This feature can help you evaluate sharpness and exposure details. When you review an image, press ⊕ (located on back of the camera in the top right corner) repeatedly to progressively magnify the image. Press ⊞·⊖ (located immediately to the left of ⊕), to reduce the magnification. You can quickly return to full size by pushing ▶.

Use ✧ to move the magnified image around within the LCD monitor in order to look at different sections of the picture. The Main dial ⌂ moves from one image to another at the same magnified view so you can compare the sharpness of a particular detail, for example.

Note: You do not have to be in the basic information display mode to use the magnify feature. For example, if you are viewing the display with full shooting information, press ⊕ to move all the data off the screen and zoom into the image.

Erasing Files

The Rebel T1i's process for erasing photos and videos from the memory card is the same as that used by most digital cameras: You can erase files during playback or right after capture when an image appears in review. With the image displayed on the LCD monitor, push 🗑. A screen appears with two options: [Cancel], which exits without deleting, and [Erase], which immediately erases the displayed file. Highlight the appropriate choice and press ⊛. The ⊒ menu also offers a way to delete either all your files, or more than one file at a time.

Note: Once a file is erased, it is gone for good. Make sure you no longer want an image or video before making the decision to erase it.

Image Protection

I consider this feature to be one of a digital camera's most underused and under-appreciated functions. At first, it seems like no big deal—why protect your images? You take care of the memory card and promptly download files to the safety of your computer.

But that's not what image protection is about. Its most important function is to allow you to go through your pictures one at a time on the LCD monitor, choosing which ones to keep, or "protect," meaning all the rest can be discarded.

Protection is easy to apply. Go to ⊐ and select [Protect images]. Press ⊛ and an image displays in the LCD monitor with a key symbol next to the word [SET] at the top left of the photo. Go through your photos one by one using either ◄► or the ⌂. Push ⊛ for every image that is a potential keeper. A small key icon ⊡ appears in the information bar at the top of the LCD monitor. Press **MENU** to exit after protecting the desired image files.

Once you have chosen the protected images, highlight [Erase images] in ⊐, and again press ⊛. In the Erase images submenu, highlight [All images on card] and once more press ⊛. A screen displays reminding you that you are about to erase all the images on the memory card except those that have been protected. Highlight [OK] and press ⊛. All the images on the card are erased except the protected ones. You have now performed a quick edit, giving you fewer photos to download and deal with on the computer.

Note: There is often downtime when shooting. Use it to select photos and movies to edit by protecting key shots. However, it is important to realize that protecting images in this way does not safeguard them from the "Format" function. When the camera formats the card, all of the data on the card is erased.

TV Playback

In order to display your images and movies, the T1i has both an analog video and audio output, and an HDMI connector. Use the supplied cable for analog output to an analog television. Most HDTVs have an HDMI input. The T1i uses a mini HDMI connector, so you'll have to purchase an HDMI-to-HDMI mini-cable. You can find this cable at electronics retailers or you can purchase the Canon cable HTC-100.

Note: The analog and HDMI outputs cannot be used simultaneously. Also, when you use either video output, the LCD monitor remains off.

If a group of people need to see your photos and you have access to a television with a standard RCA video input connection, you can display images from the memory card on the TV. If you travel you may need to change the video system in order to playback onto a television. First, go to the Set-up 2 menu ✔: and select the option [Video system]. If you are in North America, be sure to choose NTSC. (In many other parts of the world, you need to select PAL.) Make sure both the camera and television are turned off, and then connect the camera to the TV. Turn the TV on, then the camera. Now press ▶ and the image appears on the TV (but not on the back of the camera).

Note: Some TVs may cut off the edges of the image.

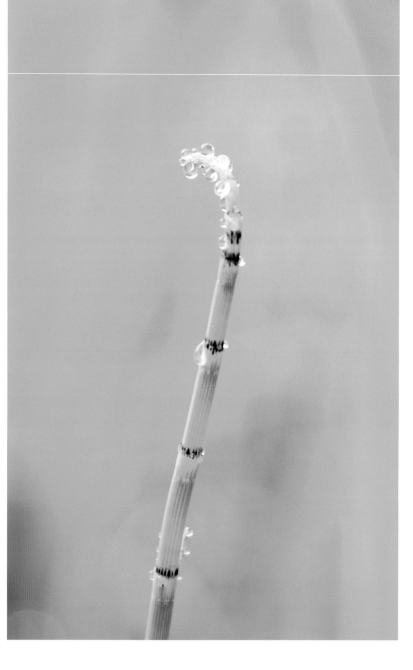

File Processing and Formats

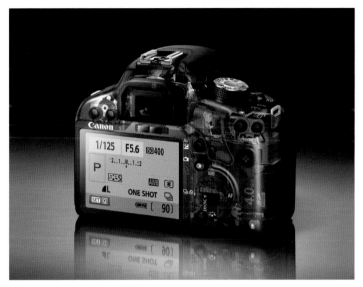

The T1i is part camera part computer. While the image sensor is an important part of image quality, equally important is image processing.

Canon has long had exceptionally strong in-camera process-ing capabilities because of their unique DIGIC Imaging Engine (DIGIC for short). The reason the Rebel T1i delivers such exceptional JPEG images is that Canon's latest version of their high-performance processor, called DIGIC 4, builds on the technology from its predecessors.

The Rebel T1i's improved DIGIC 4 processor makes it easier to cap-ture better tonal details, such as the highlights in the water droplets in the image shown here.

The DIGIC 4 processor intelligently translates the image signal as it comes from the sensor, optimizing that signal as it is converted into digital data. In essence, it is like having your own computer expert making the best possible adjustments as the data file is processed for you. DIGIC 4 works on the image in-camera, after the shutter is clicked and before the image is recorded to the memory card, improving color balance, reducing noise, refining tonalities in the brightest areas, and more. In these ways it has the potential to make JPEG files superior to unprocessed RAW files, reducing the need for RAW processing (see pages 110 for more information about JPEG and RAW files).

It is amazing that the DIGIC 4 can handle data so fast that it does not impede camera speed. The Rebel T1i has a single chip with image data processing that is appreciably faster than earlier units. Color reproduction of highly saturated, bright objects is also considerably improved. Auto white balance is better, especially at low color temperatures (such as tungsten light). In addition, false colors and noise, which have always been a challenge of digital photography, have been reduced (something that RAW files cannot offer). The ability to resolve detail in highlights is also improved.

DIGIC 4 also improves the Rebel T1i's ability to write image data to the memory card in both JPEG and RAW, which enables the camera to utilize the benefits offered by high-speed memory cards. It is important to understand that this does not affect how quickly the camera can take pictures. Rather, it affects how fast it can transfer images from its buffer (special temporary memory in the camera) to the card. It won't change the shots per second, but it will improve the quantity of images that can be taken in succession.

Speed

There are factors, however, that do affect how many shots per second the camera can take. Having a high-megapixel sensor with its comparatively large amount of data has usually meant a slower camera. Yet, this is not true of the Rebel T1i. It can take pictures at a speedy 3.4 frames per second (fps). Even at maximum resolution, the camera has a burst duration of 170 JPEG or 9 RAW frames, or 4 RAW + Large/Fine JPEGs (this occurs only with the fastest memory cards).

During Continuous shooting drive mode, each image is placed into a buffer before it is recorded to the memory card. The faster the memory card is, the faster the buffer is emptied, allowing more images to be taken in sequence. If the buffer becomes full, **buSY** appears in the viewfinder and the camera stops shooting until the card writing can catch up.

The camera is very fast in other mechanical aspects as well: The start-up time is 0.1 seconds—20 times faster than the original Digital Rebel and twice as fast as the XTi; lag time for shutter release is a mere 90 milliseconds (ms); and the viewfinder blackout time (when the mirror is up during shutter speeds of 1/60 and faster) is only 130 ms.

Picture Styles

In addition to the optimizing technology of DIGIC 4, you can choose a Picture Style to control how the camera performs some additional image processing. This can be especially helpful if you print image files directly from the camera without using a computer, or when you need to supply a particular type of image to a client. Some photographers compare Picture Styles to choosing a particular film for shooting. Picture Styles are applied permanently to JPEG files. (If using RAW files, the Picture Style can be changed during "processing" using Canon's Digital Photo Professional software.)

You gain access to Picture Styles by pressing the ▼ ⸚⸪ button; use ◄► or ⌂ to select the Picture Style you wish to use. Then press ⊛ to save the selection. There are six preset Picture styles and three user defined styles:

Standard ⸚⸪S

This is the default style for all the Basic Zone modes (see page 137) except Portrait and Landscape. During in-camera processing, color saturation is enhanced and a moderate amount of sharpening is performed on the image. Standard offers a vivid and crisp image with a normal amount of contrast.

Portrait ⸚⸪P

This is the selected mode for Portrait 🕺 in the Basic Zone. It places an emphasis on pleasing skin tones. While the contrast is the same as Standard, skin tones have a slightly warmer look. Sharpening is reduced in order to produce a pleasing soft skin texture.

Landscape ⸚⸪L

This is the selected mode for Landscape ⛰ in the Basic Zone. Saturation is high, with an emphasis on blues and greens. There is also a boost in saturation in the yellows. The image is sharpened even more than the Standard mode to display details. Don't be afraid to use this during cloudy days to help bring out more color.

Neutral ⸚⸪N

If you plan to "process" the image on your computer either through Canon's Digital Photo Professional software or some other image software program, this may be the mode to choose. There is virtually no image sharpening. Color saturation is lower than other modes and contrast is lower, too. Since other picture styles increase saturation, Neutral may be a good style to choose when you shoot in bright or high-contrast situations. Picture details may be more prevalent with this setting. Don't rule it out for candid portraits that might occur in bright lighting situations.

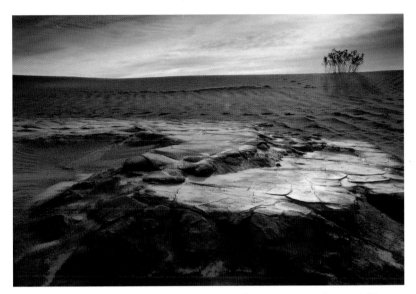

Use the Landscape style to automatically process an image with increased saturation and sharpness.

Faithful ⌗⌗F

This is the choice when you need to accurately capture the colors in the scene. Saturation is low and almost no sharpening is applied to the image. Contrast is also toned down. Accurate color reproduction is achieved when the scene is lit with 5200K lighting. Otherwise you might think of this setting as similar to Neutral, except that the color tone is a bit warmer. Like Neutral, this mode is designed with further image processing via computer in mind.

Monochrome ⌗⌗M

This allows you to record pure black-and-white images to the memory card and to automatically view the image in black-and-white on the LCD. Sharpness is the same as the Standard mode and contrast is enhanced. As with the other Picture Styles, Monochrome permanently changes JPEG files—you can't get the color back. Another option is to shoot in color and convert images to black and white in an image-processing program—and do so with more control.

With all of the Picture Styles (except Monochrome), you can control the degree of processing applied to four aspects of an image:

- [Sharpness] refers to the amount of sharpening that is applied to the image file by the camera.
- [Contrast] increases or decreases the contrast of the scene that is captured by the camera.
- [Saturation] influences color richness or intensity.
- [Color tone] helps the photographer decide how red or how yellow to render skin tones, but also affects other colors.

For Monochrome (black-and-white), the parameters are [Sharpness], [Contrast], [Filter effect], and [Toning effect].

Use ◑⋮ to modify Picture Styles. Highlight [Picture Style] and then press ⊛. A list of all the Picture Styles is presented, along with a series of numbers representing the current parameter settings for each style. Parameter numbers displayed in blue indicate a setting that has been changed from the default setting.

Note: While the ▼ ⋧⋮⋦ key is the fastest way to select a picture style, you can also use this submenu screen to select one. Just highlight the style you wish to use and press ⊛. The picture style currently in use is in blue.

Scroll to highlight the Picture Style you wish to modify. Press DISP. to enter the [Detail set.] submenu. (To return to the Menu screen at any time, press MENU.)

The [Detail set.] submenu allows you to further adjust the styles. [Sharpness], [Contrast], [Saturation], and [Color tone] are represented by a selection point on a slider-type scale. With the exception of [Sharpness], the default setting is 0 (no user changes).

Each Picture Style parameter is flexible. Use ▲▼ to select the parameter that you want to adjust. Press ⊛ to enter adjustment mode. A white pointer shows the current setting. The gray pointer shows the default setting for that style. Use ◀▶ to adjust the parameter. You must use ⊛ to accept the setting. If you leave this menu screen without pressing ⊛, the adjustment is cancelled. There is also the [Default set] option at the bottom of the screen accessed by ▲▼. Use this to reset the Picture Style to its factory setting. Use MENU to return to the Picture Style menu.

The adjustment slider for [Sharpness] is set up differently than the other sliders. Sharpness is generally required at some point in digital photography. It overcomes, among other things, the use of a low-pass filter in front of the image sensor (to reduce problems caused by the image sensor's pixel grid). The low-pass filter introduces a small amount of image blur and image sharpening compensates for this blur. The adjustment slider's setting indicates the amount of sharpness already applied to the style. A setting of zero means that almost no sharpening has been applied to the image. You'll notice that the [Sharpness] parameter's default setting is the only one that changes from Picture Style to Picture Style.

With the Monochrome Picture Style, the [Saturation] and [Color tone] settings are replaced with [Filter effect] and [Toning effect]. The parameters for [Filter effect] offer four tonal effects that mimic what a variety of colored filters do to black-and-white film (see below). A fifth setting, N:None, means that no filter effects are applied. Each Filter effect color choice makes the color similar to your selection look lighter, while the color opposite your selection on the color wheel records darker. The Monochrome Filter effects are:

- Ye:Yellow is a modest effect that darkens skies slightly and gives what many black-and-white aficionados consider the most natural looking grayscale image.

- Or:Orange is next in intensity. It does what red does, only to a lesser degree. It is better explained if you understand the use of red (see next description).

- R:Red is dramatic, lightening anything that is red, such as flowers or ruddy skin tones, while darkening blues and greens. Skies turn quite striking and sunlit scenes gain in contrast (the sunny areas are warm-toned and the shadows are cool-toned, so the warms get lighter and the cools get darker).

- G:Green makes Caucasian skin tones look more natural and foliage gets bright and lively in tone.

Of course, the great thing about shooting with the Rebel T1i is that if you aren't sure what these filters will do, you can take the picture and see the effect immediately on the LCD monitor.

The other Monochrome parameter, [Toning effect], adds color to the black-and-white image so it looks like a toned black-and-white print. Your choices include: N:None, S:Sepia, B:Blue, P:Purple, and G:Green. Sepia and blue are the tones we are most accustomed to seeing in such prints.

User-Defined Picture Styles ▨

The T1i allows you to utilize a particular Picture Style as a base setting and modify it to meet your own photographic needs. This allows you to create and register a different set of parameters you can apply to image files while keeping the preset Picture Styles. You do this under the options for [User Def. 1], [User Def. 2], or [User Def. 3].

While specific situations may affect where you place your control points for these flexible options, here are some suggestions to consider:

- Create a hazy or cloudy day setting: Make one of the user-defined sets capture more contrast and color on days when contrast and color are weak. Increase the scale for

Contrast and Saturation by one or two points (experiment to see what you like when you open the files on your computer or use the camera for direct printing). You can also increase the red setting of Color tone (adjust the scale to the left).

- Create a portrait setting: Make a set that favors skin tones. Start with the Portrait style as your base, then reduce Contrast by one point while increasing Saturation by one point (this is very subjective—some photographers may prefer less saturation) and warming skin tones (by moving Color tone toward the red—or left—side) by one point.

- Create a Velvia (an intensely colored slide film) look: Start with Standard style, increase Contrast two points, Sharpness one point, and Saturation by two points.

You can also download custom picture styles from Canon's Picture Style website:

http://web.canon.jp/imaging/picturestyle/index.html

These custom styles can be uploaded into any of the T1i's three User-defined fields by using the USB connection to the camera. (Requires Canon's EOS Utility software that is included with the camera.) The custom styles can also be used with Canon's Digital Photo Professional software to change styles after-the-fact in RAW images.

Note: Downloaded Picture Styles can only be loaded into the User-defined styles and are deleted if you reset all camera settings using [Clear settings] in ♥:.

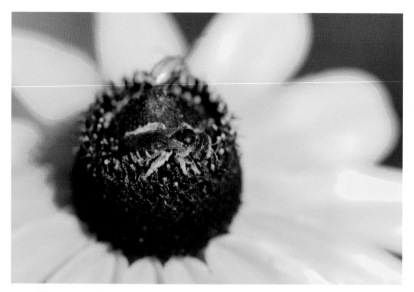

Choose a color space that will best reproduce your images; sRGB works well for images intended for the web, and Adobe RGB is a good choice for images that will be printed.

Color Space

The T1i has a color space setting in the ⚙ menu. A color space is the range of colors or gamut that a device can produce. Cameras have color spaces, monitors have color spaces, and printers have color spaces. (While not technically accurate, you can think of different color spaces as different sized boxes of crayons.)

The two choices for color space on the T1i are sRGB and Adobe RGB. sRGB is the default setting for the camera and is used as the color space for the Basic Zone modes. It is also the color space for most computer monitors. If you are capturing images for the web, sRGB will work fine. Adobe RGB, as the name implies, was developed by Adobe to deal with printers. This larger color space (think bigger box of crayons) contains most of the colors that can be produced by today's printers.

Choosing between sRGB and Adobe RGB is not as complicated as JPEG vs. RAW. Adobe RGB doesn't take up more room on the card or require special RAW processing software. But you do need to check to make sure that your image-processing program can handle Adobe RGB—most do.

There are many times when it is difficult to see the difference between the two color spaces. Try an experiment with some test shots in both. You won't see the difference on the LCD, so print them out and then see if you can tell the difference. Since your images may outlast today's printers, I recommend that you shoot with Adobe RGB.

Note: When using Adobe RGB, image file names begin with "_MG" rather than "IMG".

White Balance

White balance (WB) is an important digital camera control. It addresses a problem that has plagued film photographers for ages: How to deal with the different color temperatures of various light sources. While color adjustments can be made in the computer after shooting, especially when shooting RAW, there is a definite benefit to setting white balance properly from the start. The Rebel T1i helps you do this with an improved Auto white balance **AWB** setting that makes colors more accurate and natural than earlier D-SLRs. In addition, improved algorithms and the DIGIC 4 processor make **AWB** more stable as you shoot a scene from different angles and focal lengths (which is always a challenge when using this setting). Further, white balance has been improved to make color reproduction more accurate under low lights.

While **AWB** gives excellent results in a number of situations, many photographers find they prefer the control offered by presets and custom WB settings. With eight separate white balance settings, plus white balance compensation and bracketing, the Rebel T1i's ability to carefully control color balance is greatly enhanced. It is well worth the effort to learn how to use the different white balance functions so you can get the best color with the most efficient workflow in all situations (including RAW). This is especially important in strongly colored scenes, such as sunrise or sunset, which can fool **AWB**.

The preset WB settings are simple enough to learn that they should become part of the photography decision-making process. However, they can only be used with the Creative Zone exposure modes (see pages 140-148). The more involved Custom white balance setting ⊾⊿ is also a valuable tool to understand and use so you can capture the truest color in all conditions (see pages 104-107).

To set white balance when there are no menus displayed on the LCD, press the ▲ WB button found on the back of the camera to the right of the LCD. A list of WB choices appears. Next, use ◄► or ⌒ to choose the white balance setting you want, then press ⊛. The information display on the LCD monitor shows an icon of the white balance setting that you selected.

White balance settings fall within certain color temperature values, corresponding to a measurement of how cool (blue) or warm (red) the light source in the scene is. The measurement is in degrees Kelvin, abbreviated as K. Unlike air temperature, the higher the number, the "cooler" the light source. Conversely, the lower the number, the warmer the light source.

White Balance Presets

Auto **AWB** (Color temperature range of approximately 3000–7000K): This setting examines the scene for you, interprets the light it sees (in the range denoted above) using the DIGIC 4 processor (even with RAW), compares the conditions to what Canon's engineers have determined works for such readings, and sets a white balance to make colors look neutral (i.e., whites appear pure, without color casts, and skin tones appear normal).

Auto can be a useful setting when you move quickly from one type of light to another, or whenever you hope to get neutral colors and need to shoot fast. Even if it isn't the perfect setting for all conditions, it often gets you close enough so that only a little adjustment is needed later using your image-processing software. However, if you have time, it is often better to choose from the white balance settings listed below, because colors are more consistent from picture to picture. While Auto is well designed, it can only interpret how it "thinks" a scene should look. If the camera sees your wide-angle and telephoto shots of the same subject differently in terms of colors, it will readjust for each shot, often resulting in inconsistent color from shot to shot.

Daylight ☀ (approximately 5200K): This setting adjusts the camera to make colors appear natural when you shoot in sunlit situations between about 10 A.M. and 4 P.M. (middle of the day). At other times, when the sun is lower in the sky and has more red light, the scenes photographed using this setting appear warmer than normally seen with our eyes. This setting makes indoor scenes under incandescent lights look very warm.

Shade 🏠 (approximately 7000K): Shadowed subjects under blue skies can end up very bluish in tone, so this setting warms the light to make colors look natural, without any blue color cast. (At least that's the ideal—individual situations affect how the setting performs.) The Shade setting is a good one to use any time you want to warm up a scene (especially when people are included), but you have to experiment to see how you like this creative use of the setting.

Cloudy ☁ (approximately 6000K): Even though the symbol for this setting is a cloud, you might think of it as the Cloudy/twilight/sunset setting. It warms up cloudy scenes as if you had a warming filter, making sunlight appear warm, but not quite to the degree that the Shade setting does. You may prefer the Cloudy setting to Shade when shooting people, since the effect is not as strong. Both settings actually work well for sunrise and sunset, giving the warm colors that we expect to see in such photographs. However, the Cloudy setting offers a slightly weaker effect. You really have to experiment a bit when using these settings for creative effect. Make the final comparisons on the computer.

Tungsten light ☀ **(approximately 3200K):** Tungsten light is designed to give natural results with quartz lights. (The term "tungsten" comes from the name of the metal that makes up the filament in light bulbs.) It also reduces the strong orange color that is typical when photographing lamp-lit indoor scenes with daylight-balanced settings. Since this control adds a cold tone to other conditions, it can also be used creatively for this purpose (to make a snow scene appear bluer, for example).

White fluorescent light ☷ **(approximately 4000K):** The **AWB** setting often works well with fluorescents but, under many conditions, the White fluorescent light setting is more precise and predictable. Fluorescent lights usually appear green in photographs, so this setting adds magenta to neutralize that effect. (Since fluorescents can be extremely variable, and since the Rebel T1i has only one fluorescent choice, you may find that precise color can only be achieved with the Custom white balance setting.) You can also use this setting creatively any time you wish to add a warm pinkish tone to your photo (such as during sunrise or sunset).

Flash ⚡ **(approximately 6000K):** Light from flash tends to be a little colder than daylight, so this warms it up. According to Canon tech folks, this setting is essentially the same as Cloudy (the Kelvin temperature is the same); it is simply labeled differently to make it easy to remember and use. I actually use both Flash and Cloudy a lot, finding them to be good, all-around settings that give a slight but attractive warm tone to outdoor scenes.

Custom White Balance ◲

A very important tool for the digital photographer, Custom white balance is a setting that even pros often don't fully understand. It is a precise and adaptable way of getting

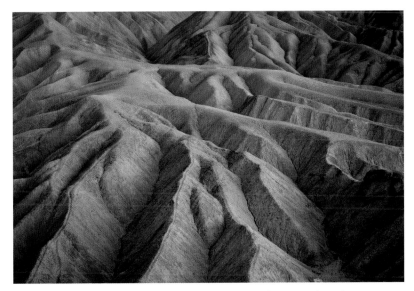

Auto white balance will attempt to remove color casts from images. If you want a specific look, such as more blue in a landscape as shown here, experiment with the white balance presets.

accurate or creative white balance. It has no specific white balance K temperature, but is set based on a specific neutral tone in the light in the scene to be photographed. However, it deals with a significantly wider range than Auto (between approximately 2000–10,000K). That can be very useful.

The Custom setting lets you choose a white (or gray) target on which the camera sets white balance.

Hint: I like to use a card or paper with black print on it rather than a plain white card. This way, if I can see the type, I haven't overexposed the image.

First, take a picture of something white (or a known neutral tone) that is in the same light as your subject. You can use a piece of paper or a gray card. It does not have to be in focus, but it should fill the image area. (Avoid placing the card on or near a highly reflective colored surface.) Be sure the exposure is set to make this object gray to light gray in tone, and not dark (underexposed) or washed out white (overexposed).

Next, go to 📷, highlight [Custom WB], and press ⊛. The last shot you took (the one for white balance) should be displayed in the LCD monitor. If not, use ◀▶ to choose the image you shot of the white or gray object.

When you have the target image displayed in the LCD monitor, push ⊛. A dialog box asks you if you want to use the white balance information from the current image to set a custom white balance. Highlight [OK], press ⊛, and the Custom white balance is set to measure that stored shot. A note appears, "Set WB to ◣◼◢," as a reminder. This reminds you that there is one more step in this process: You must choose the ◣◼◢ setting for white balance.

To take that final step, press ⊛ again to acknowledge the reminder, and then either lightly tap the shutter or press MENU to exit 📷. Then press the ▲ WB button and select ◣◼◢. Of course, don't forget to lock in the selection with ⊛. The camera is now set for your Custom white balance.

You may save a series of white balance reference images on your memory card ahead of time that you can flip through. This is useful if you need to switch between different lighting conditions but don't have the time to set up a card to capture the image.

The procedure just described produces neutral colors in some very difficult conditions. However, if the color of the lighting is mixed, like a situation where the subject is lit on one side by a window and on the other by incandescent lights, you will only get neutral colors for the light that the white card was in. Also, when shooting in reduced spectrum lights—such as sodium vapor—you will not get a neutral white under any white balance setting.

You can also use Custom white balance to create special color for a scene. In this case, you white balance on a color that is not white or gray. You can use a pale blue, for example, to generate a nice amber color. If you balance on the blue, the camera adjusts this color to neutral, which in essence removes blue, so the scene has an amber cast. Different strengths of blue provide varied results. You can use any color you want for white balancing—the camera works to remove (or reduce) that color, which means the opposite color becomes stronger. (For example, using a pale magenta increases the green response.)

White Balance Correction
The Rebel T1i goes beyond the capabilities of many cameras in offering control over white balance: There is actually a white-balance correction feature built into the camera. You might think of this as exposure compensation for white balance. It is like having a set of color balancing filters in four colors (blue, amber, green, and magenta) and in varied strengths. Photographers accustomed to using color conversion or color correction filters will find this feature quite helpful in getting just the right color.

The setting is not difficult to manage. First, go to ◘⁞, highlight [WB SHIFT/BKT] and press ⊛. A menu screen appears with a graph that has a horizontal axis from blue to amber (left to right) and a vertical axis from green to magenta (top to bottom). You move a selection point within that graph using the cross keys. As you change the position of the selection point on the graph, an alphanumeric display titled [SHIFT] on the right of the screen shows a letter for the color (B, A, G, or M) and a number for the setting. For example, a white balance shift of three steps toward blue and four to green displays B3 and G4.

For photographers used to color-balancing filters, each increment of color adjustment equals 5 MIREDS of a color-temperature changing filter. (A MIRED is a measuring unit for the strength of a color temperature conversion filter.) Remember to set the correction back to zero when conditions change. The LCD monitor and the viewfinder information display show ⚞ when white-balance correction is engaged.

White Balance Auto Bracketing

When you run into a difficult lighting situation and want to be sure of the best possible white balance settings, another option is white balance auto bracketing. This is actually quite different than autoexposure bracketing. With the latter, three separate exposures are taken of a scene; with white balance auto bracketing, you take just one exposure and the camera processes it to give you three different white balance options.

Note: Using white balance bracketing delays the recording of images to the memory card. In other words, the burst mode of the camera is reduced and the number of shots in a row is one-third the normal number. Pay attention to the access lamp in the bottom right corner of the back of the T1i to gauge when the camera is finished recording the extra images.

White balance auto bracketing allows up to +/- 3 levels (again, each step is equal to 5 MIREDS of a color correction filter) and is based on whatever white balance mode you have currently selected. You can bracket from blue to amber or from green to magenta. Keep in mind that even at the strongest settings, the color changes are fairly subtle. ⚞ on the LCD monitor appears to let you know that white balance auto bracketing is set.

To access white balance auto bracketing, go to ◻: and select [WB SHIFT/BKT], then press ⬢. The graph screen with the horizontal (blue/amber) and vertical (green/magenta) axes appears on the LCD monitor. Rotate ⌇ to adjust the bracketing amount: To the right (clockwise) to set the blue/amber adjustment, then back to zero and go to the left (counter clockwise) for green/magenta. (You can't bracket in both directions.) You can also shift your setting from the center point of the graph by using ✧. Press ⬢ to accept your settings.

Note: White balance bracketing records an original image at the currently selected white balance setting, then internally creates an additional set of (1) a bluer image and a more amber image, or (2) a more magenta and a greener image. Unlike exposure bracketing, you only need to take one shot—and you don't have to set the drive setting to ▣.

The obvious use of this feature is to deal with tricky lighting conditions. However, it has other uses as well. You may want to add a warm touch to a portrait but are not sure how strong you want it. You could set the white balance to ☁, for example, then use white balance auto bracketing to get the tone you're looking for. (The bracketing gives you the standard ☁ white-balanced shot, plus versions warmer and cooler than that.) Or, you may run into a situation where the light changes from one part of the image to another. Here, you can shoot the bracket, then combine the white balance versions using an image-processing program. (Take the nicely white-balanced parts of one bracketed photograph and combine them with a different bracketed shot that has good white balance in the areas that were lacking in the first photo.)

RAW and White Balance

Since the RAW file format (see following pages) allows you to change white balance after the shot, some photographers have come to believe that it is not important to select an appropriate white balance at the time the photo is taken. While it is true that **AWB** and RAW give excellent results in many situations, this approach can cause consistency and workflow challenges. White balance choice is important because when you bring RAW files into software for processing and enhancement, the files open with the settings that you chose during initial image capture. Sure, you can edit those settings in the computer, but why not make your initial RAW image better by merely tweaking the white balance with minor revisions at the image-processing stage rather than starting from an image that requires major correction? Of course there will be times that getting a good white balance setting is difficult, and this is when the RAW software white balance correction can really be a big help.

File Formats

The Rebel T1i records images as either JPEG or RAW files. There has been a mistaken notion that JPEG is a file format for amateur photographers while RAW is a format for professionals. This is really not the case. Pros use JPEG and some amateurs use RAW. (Technically, JPEG is a compression scheme and not a format, but the term is commonly used to denote format and that is how we will use it.)

There is no question that RAW offers some distinct benefits for the photographer who needs them, including the ability to make greater changes to the image file before the image degrades from over-processing. The Rebel T1i's RAW format (called CR2 and originally developed by Canon for the EOS-1D Mark II) includes revised processing improvements, making it more flexible and versatile for photographers than previous versions. It can also handle more metadata and can store processing parameters for future use.

However, RAW is not for everyone. It requires more work and more time to process than other formats. For the photographer who likes to work quickly and wants to spend less time at the computer, JPEG may offer clear advantages, and with the Rebel T1i, even give better results. This might sound radical considering what some "experts" say about RAW in relation to JPEG, but I suspect they have never shot an image with an EOS Rebel T1i set for high-quality JPEGs.

It is important to understand how the sensor processes an image. It sees a certain range of tones coming to it from the lens. Too much light (overexposed), and the detail washes out; too little light (underexposed), and the picture is dark. This is analog (continuous) information, and it must be converted to digital, which is true for any file format, including both RAW and JPEG. The complete digital data is based on 14 bits of color information, which is changed to 8-bit color data for JPEG, or simply placed virtually unchanged into a 16-bit file for RAW. (The fact that RAW files contain 14-bit color information is a little confusing since this information

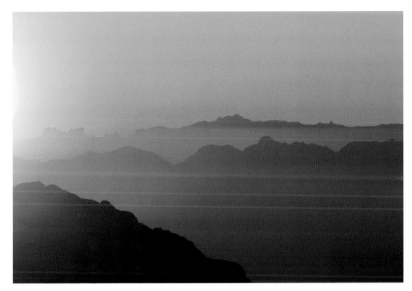

The image file size you choose is important; it determines how much data is saved from the sensor. If you know in advance that you want to reproduce images as prints, you should always use the largest image file size.

is put into a file that is actually a 16-bit format.) This occurs for each of three different color channels used by the Rebel T1i: red, green, and blue. Remember that the DIGIC 4 processor applies changes to JPEG files, while RAW files have very little processing applied by the camera.

Note: A bit is the smallest piece of information that a computer uses—an acronym for binary digit. Data of eight bits or higher are required for true photographic color.

Both 8-bit and 16-bit files have the same range from pure white to pure black because that range is influenced only by the capability of the sensor. If the sensor cannot capture detail in areas that are too bright or too dark, then a RAW file cannot deliver that detail any better than a JPEG file. It is true that RAW allows greater technical control over an image than JPEG, primarily because it starts with more data (14 bits in a 16-bit file), meaning there are more "steps" of information between the

111

white and black extremes of the sensor's sensitivity range. These steps are especially evident in the darkest and lightest areas of the photo. So it appears the RAW file has more exposure latitude and that greater adjustment to the image is possible before banding or color tearing becomes noticeable.

JPEG format compresses (or reduces) the size of the image file, allowing more pictures to fit on a memory card. The JPEG algorithms carefully look for redundant data in the file (such as a large area of a single color) and remove it, while keeping instructions on how to reconstruct the file. JPEG is therefore referred to as a lossy format because, technically, data is lost. The computer rebuilds the lost data quite well as long as the amount of compression is low.

It is essential to note that both RAW and JPEG files can give excellent results. Photographers who shoot both (RAW+◢L) use the flexibility of RAW files to deal with tough exposure situations, and the convenience of JPEG files when they need fast and easy handling of images.

Which format will work best for you? Your own personal way of shooting and working should dictate that. If you deal with problem lighting and colors, for example, RAW gives you a lot of flexibility in controlling both. If you can carefully control your exposures and keep images consistent, JPEG is more efficient.

Processing RAW Files
In addition to the fact that it holds 14 bits of data, the RAW file offers some advantages over JPEG. Because RAW more directly captures what the sensor sees, stronger correction can be applied to it (compared to JPEG images) without problems appearing. This can be particularly helpful when there are difficulties with exposure or color balance.

The disadvantage to RAW files is that you must process the image using RAW processing software on your computer.

Canon supplies a dedicated software program with the Rebel T1i called ZoomBrowser EX (Windows) or Image-Browser (Mac). Both programs are specifically designed for CR2 files and allow you to open and smartly process them. You can also choose other processing programs, such as Phase One's Capture One or others, which make converting from RAW files easier. These independent software programs are intended for professional use and can be expensive (although some manufacturers offer less expensive solutions).

One disadvantage to using third-party programs is that they may not support Canon's Dust Delete Data system to automatically remove dust artifacts in your images. Also, Picture Styles may not be supported in software other than Canon's.

Whatever method you choose to gain access to RAW files in your computer, you have excellent control over the images in terms of exposure and color of light. The RAW file contains special metadata (shooting information stored by the camera) that has the exposure settings you selected at the time of shooting. The RAW conversion program uses this data when it opens an image. You can make modifications to the exposure without causing too much harm to the image. (However, you can't compensate for really bad exposure in the first place.) White balance settings can also be changed. If you use Canon's software you can even change Picture Styles after the fact.

Image Size and Quality

The Rebel T1i offers a total of eight choices for image-recording quality, consisting of combinations of different file formats, resolutions (number of pixels), and compression rates. But let's be straight about this: Most photographers will shoot the maximum image size using RAW or the high-est-quality JPEG setting. There is little point in shooting smaller image sizes except for specialized purposes. After all, the camera's high resolution is what you paid for!

All settings for recording quality are selected in the ⌂˙ menu under [Quality]. Press ⊛ to make the different quality options appear, designated by a symbol and a letter. The symbols depict the level of compression; the letter stands for the resolution size of the image file. You can't set compression level or size on RAW files.

You can see what your image size is currently set for with the Quick Control screen.

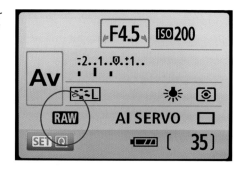

Note: Don't forget, you always use the Quick Control Screen to set image size and quality.

The symbol with the smooth curve represents the lesser amount of compression (Fine = better quality), and when combined with L (large resolution size), makes a very high quality image. The symbol with a stair shape illustrates higher compression (Normal = lesser quality), giving a good quality JPEG image, but not as good as the Fine setting.

The most useful settings are ◢L (the largest image size for JPEG, 15.1 megapixels, resulting in an approximate file size of 5.0MB) and ██ (always 15.1 megapixels; since it is uncompressed, no compression symbol is displayed; it results in an approximate file size of 20.2MB).

Note: Near the top of the Quality menu is a status line that shows the current selection, the size of the image file in megapixels, the dimensions of the image file in pixels, and the number of images—at the current image-recording quality—that will fit in the space that is currently available on the memory card.

The Rebel T1i can record both RAW and JPEG simultaneously. Designated **RAW**+▲**L**, this option can be useful for photographers who want added flexibility. It records images using the same name prefix, but with different formats designated by their extensions: .JPG for JPEG and .CR2 for RAW. You can then use the JPEG file, for example, for printing at a photo kiosk, sending to a friend, and taking advantage of the DIGIC 4 processor. And you still have the RAW file for use when you need its added processing power. (The **RAW**+▲**L** setting cannot be used in the Basic Zone.)

If you find yourself frequently switching between quality settings, you can set Custom Function 11 (C.Fn 11; see page 79) to change the functionality of ⊛. When this function is utilized, you won't have to press **MENU** to call up the display and then navigate to [Quality]. You simply press ⊛ and the Quality menu appears on the LCD monitor. Then it is just a matter of selecting the desired item by pressing ⊛ and you can start shooting at the new setting.

Note: If you change ⊛ to operate this way, you will not be able to use ⊛ to activate the Quick Control Screen.

The RAW file initially appears in your RAW conversion software with the same processing details as the JPEG file (including white balance, color matrix, and exposure), all of which can be altered in the RAW software. Though RAW is adaptable, it is not magic. You are still limited by the original exposure, as well as by the tonal and color capabilities of the sensor. Using RAW is not an excuse to become sloppy in your shooting simply because it gives you more options to control the look of your images. If you do not capture the best possible file, your results will be less than the camera is capable of producing.

Each recording quality choice influences how many photos can fit on a memory card. Most photographers shoot with large memory cards because they want the space required by the high-quality files available on this camera. It is impossible to give exact numbers of how many JPEG images fit on a card because this compression technology is variable. You can change the compression as needed (resulting in varied file sizes), but remember that JPEG compresses each file differently depending on what is in the photo and how it can be compressed. For example, a photo with a lot of detail does not compress as much as an image with a large area of solid color.

The following chart gives you an idea of how large these files are and how many images might fit on a 2GB memory card. The figures are based on actual numbers produced by the camera using such a card. (JPEG values are always approximate.) Also, the camera uses some space on the card for its own purposes and for file management, so you do not have access to the entire 2GB capacity for image files.

You can immediately see one advantage that JPEG gives over RAW: Even if you use the highest-quality JPEG file at the full 15.1 megapixels, you can store nearly four times the number of JPEGs compared to RAW.

Image Size and Card Capacity Based on 2GB Memory Card

Quality	Megapixels	File Size	Possible Shots	Max Burst (Approx MB)
RAW+◢L (High)	Approx 15.1	20.2 + 5.0	72	4
RAW (High)	Approx 15.1	20.2	90	9
◢L (High)	Approx 15.1	5.0	370	170
◢L (High)	Approx 15.1	2.5	740	740
◢M (Medium)	Approx 8.0	3.0	610	610
◢M (Medium)	Approx 8.0	1.6	1190	1190
◢S (Small)	Approx 3.7	1.7	1080	1080
◢S (Small)	Approx 3.7	0.9	2030	2030

Note: All quantities are approximate based on the photographic subject, brand and type of memory card, ISO speed, and other possible factors.

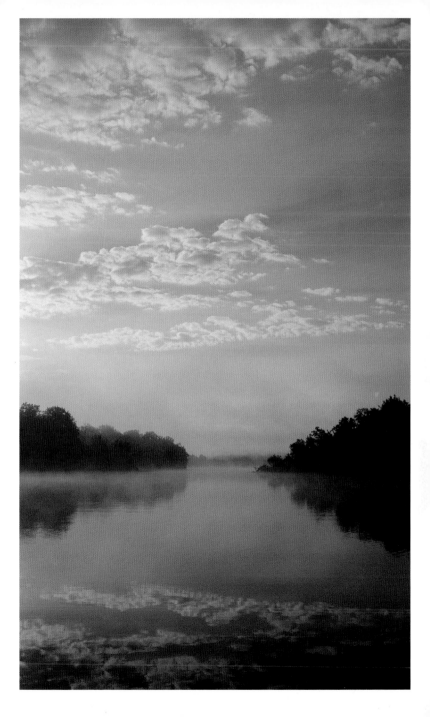

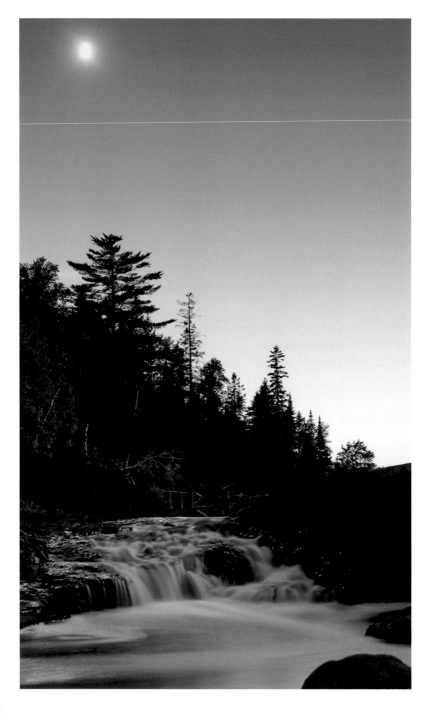

Camera Operation Modes

The innovation, thought, and technology that have gone into the T1i become evident as soon as you begin to operate its various systems and utilize its many functions. Clearly the Rebel T1i is a highly sophisticated camera. From finding focus on moving subjects, to shooting multiple frames per second, to capturing great exposures in low light, the Rebel T1i offers a number of options that enhance your ability to take excellent photographs.

Focus

The Rebel T1i uses an AI (artificial intelligence) AF (autofocus) system based on a special CMOS sensor dedicated to autofocus. The nine AF points give the camera nine distinct spots where it can measure focus. Eight points are positioned in a diamond pattern around a central ninth point. This diagonal arrangement makes for improved focus tracking of moving subjects.

The AF points work with an EV (exposure value) range of EV –0.5 to +18 (at ISO 100), and are superimposed in the viewfinder. They can be used automatically (the camera selects them as needed), or you can choose one manually.

⟲ *Finding accurate focus in dim or dark situations has been a challenge to photographers in the past, but the Rebel T1i's focusing system can handle a variety of challenging shoots.*

The Rebel T1i smartly handles various functions of autofocus through the use of a high-performance microcomputer along with improvements in AF system design. The camera's ability to autofocus while tracking a moving subject is quite good. According to Canon, for example, in AI Servo AF (continuous focus) with an EF 300mm f/2.8 IS USM lens, the Rebel T1i can focus-track a subject moving toward the camera at a speed of 31 mph (50 kph) up to about 32.8 feet (10 meters) away.

This specification doesn't just mean that the T1i can track only objects moving 31 mph (50 kph) and slower. For example, AI Servo AF can track a racecar traveling at 124 mph (200 kph) until it is about 65.6 ft (20 m) from the camera. The T1i does this by employing statistical prediction while using multiple focusing operations to follow an erratically moving subject. Even if the subject is not moving, the AI Servo AF control is notably stable—it will not allow the lens to change focus until the subject moves again.

When light levels are low, the camera activates AF-assist with the built-in flash and produces a series of quick flashes to help autofocus. (External dedicated flashes can also do this. See C.Fn 8 on page 78.) The range is up to approximately 13.1 ft (4 m) in the center of the frame and 11.5 ft (3.5 m) at the other AF points. The 580EX II Speedlite includes a more powerful AF-assist beam effective up to 32.8 ft (10 m).

AF Modes

The camera has three AF modes: One-Shot AF, AI Servo AF, and AI Focus AF. Manual focusing is also an option. In the Basic Zone modes, the AF mode is set automatically. In the Creative Zone modes, you can choose among all three settings. Access these settings by pressing ▶ AF (right cross key)—this button displays the AF mode menu on the LCD monitor. Use ◀▶ or ⚙ to select the mode you want. Once selected, press ⊛ to accept the selection. The selected AF mode is indicated on the camera settings display on the LCD monitor.

Each AF mode is used for different purposes:

One-Shot ONE SHOT: This AF mode finds and locks focus when you press the shutter button halfway. Perfect for stationary subjects, it allows you to find and hold focus on the important part of a subject. If the camera doesn't hit the right spot, simply change the framing slightly and repress the shutter button halfway to lock focus. Once you have found and locked focus, you can move the camera to set the proper composition. The focus confirmation light ● glows steadily in the viewfinder when you have locked focus. It blinks if the camera can't achieve focus. Since this camera focuses very quickly, a blinking light is a quick reminder that you need to change something (you may need to focus manually).

AI Servo AI SERVO: Great for action photography where subjects are in motion, AI Servo AF becomes active when you press the shutter button halfway, but it does not lock focus. It continually looks for the best focus as you move the camera or as the subject travels through the frame, with both the focus and exposure becoming set only at the moment of exposure. This can be a problem when used for motionless subjects because the focus continually changes, especially if you are handholding the camera. However, if you use AI Servo AF on a moving subject, it is a good idea to start the camera focusing (depressing the shutter button halfway) before you actually need to take the shot so the system can find the subject.

AI Focus AI FOCUS: This mode allows the camera to choose between **ONE SHOT** and **AI SERVO**. It can be used as the standard setting for the camera because it switches automatically from **ONE SHOT** to **AI SERVO** if your subject should start to move. Note, however, that if the subject is still—such as a landscape—this mode might detect other movement (such as a blowing tree), so it may not lock on the non-moving subject.

121

Note: Focus during Live View shooting is handled differently and is covered later in the following chapter (page 163).

Selecting an AF Point

You can let the T1i select the AF point automatically, or you can manually select a desired point. Manual AF point selection is useful when you have a specific composition in mind and the camera won't focus consistently on the desired area. To manually select an AF point, simply push the ⊞/🔍 button (on back of the camera in the upper right corner, it is also 🔍 during playback), and use ✧ or 🗫 to make the selection. Points light up in the viewfinder and on the LCD monitor as they are selected. If all points are lit, the camera automatically makes the AF point selection. You can press 🖙 to jump directly to the center AF point. Once there you can use 🖙 to toggle between the center AF point and automatic selection.

Using 🗫 rotates through all of the points and is not as direct as selecting points with ✧. However, some photographers find the dial is easier to use while looking through the viewfinder.

You can return to shooting mode at any time during AF point selection by either pressing the shutter halfway or pressing ⊞. You do not need to press 🖙 to have the camera accept your selection.

Autofocus Limitations

AF sensitivity is high with this camera. The Rebel T1i can autofocus in conditions that are quite challenging for other cameras. Still, as the maximum aperture of lenses decreases, or tele-extenders are used, the camera's AF capabilities change. AF works best with f/2.8 and wider lenses. This is normal and not a problem with the camera.

It is possible for AF to fail in certain situations, requiring you to focus manually. This is most common when the scene is low-contrast or has a continuous tone (such as sky), in conditions of extreme low light, with subjects that are

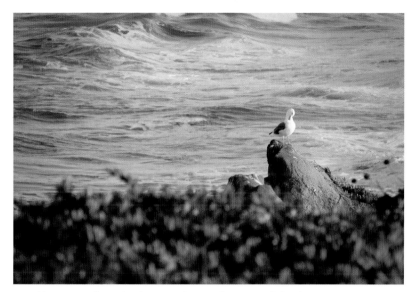

You can select the focus point on the area of the image you want in clear focus, or you can manually focus the camera to focus on your subject.

strongly backlit, and with compositions that contain repetitive patterns. A quick way to deal with these situations is to focus on something else at the same distance, lock focus on it (by keeping the shutter button pressed halfway), then move the framing back to the original composition. This only works while the camera is in **ONE SHOT** Mode.

Note: Custom Function (C.Fn) 10 can change the focus lock from the shutter release button to ✱ (see page 79).

Drive Modes and the Self-Timer

The term "drive" comes from film cameras; professional SLRs had an option to advance the film and reset the shutter with a motor drive. Even though the film is gone, mechanics are still needed in any D-SLR. The Rebel T1i offers several different drive modes, accessed by pressing the ◄⬚/♻ cross key. The Drive Mode menu displays on the LCD monitor. Use ◄► or ⚙ to highlight the drive mode you want from the menu options, and press ⊛ to accept the selection. Any drive mode that you select is indicated on the camera settings display on the LCD monitor.

Note: You can also set the drive mode using the Quick Control screen.

Single Shooting ☐: This is the standard shooting mode. One image is captured each time you press the shutter release.

Continuous Shooting ⬚: When the shutter button is held down, the camera captures at a rate of 3.4 images per second for approximately 170 consecutive JPEG images at the highest JPEG resolution and best quality. When the in-camera buffer (or the memory card) fills up, the camera stops capturing images. The camera resumes taking pictures when the buffer has space again. When you shoot RAW images a maximum of about 9 consecutive images can be captured before the buffer fills.

Self-timer/Remote Control ♻: There are actually two parts to this setting: (1) self-timer and (2) remote control. When you want to be in the picture, the 10-second self-timer is the function to use. Press the shutter button halfway and make sure you have achieved focus. Then, press the shutter release button the rest of the way down. A self-timer lamp (located on the front of the camera, built into the camera grip) flashes once a second to count down the seconds. By default, a beep is enabled and sounds during the countdown. Two seconds before the picture is taken, the lamp is solidly on and the camera beeps more frequently to let you know the shutter is about to be released. To cancel the countdown, press ◄⬚/♻.

The remote control function ☉ᵢ should be selected when you use one of Canon's optional wireless remote controls (either the RC-1 or RC-5). The RC-1 offers immediate remote shooting or after a 2-second delay. The RC-5 always has a 2-second delay.

Self-timer:2 sec ☉2: The 2-second self-timer operates similarly to the 10-second timer in that it takes the picture after a set time. When you shoot with a tripod and have longer shutter speeds, 1/60 and longer, use this quick timer, along with C.Fn 9, Mirror lockup, to reduce camera motion blur.

Self-timer:Continuous ☉c: This setting is new to the T1i. In essence it is the same as a 10-second self-timer except at the end of the countdown the camera takes multiple shots. Use ▲▼ to set the number of shots, from 2 to 10. This is a great feature for group shots where you might be concerned if someone has their eyes closed. It also can be fun to capture that moment when everyone stops posing and looks more natural.

Exposure

No matter what technology is used to create a photo, it is always preferable to have the best possible exposure. Digital photography is no exception. A properly exposed digital file is one in which the right amount of light has reached the camera's sensor and produces an image that corresponds to the scene, or to the photographer's interpretation of the scene. This applies to color reproduction, as well as tonal values and subject contrast.

ISO

ISO (sensitivity) is one control worth knowing so well that its use becomes intuitive. The first step in getting the best exposure is to provide the camera's meter with information on the sensor's sensitivity to light. The meter can then determine how much exposure is required to properly record the image. Digital cameras adjust the sensitivity of the sensor circuits to settings that can be compared to film of the same ISO speed. (This "apparent" change in sensitivity actually involves amplifying the electronic sensor data that creates the image.)

The Rebel T1i offers ISO speed settings of 100-3,200. This range can be expanded to 100-12,800 by using C.Fn 2. When expanded there are two additional speeds—6,400 and "H". However, the expanded ISO setting does not come without drawbacks. When set for ISO 6,400 or H (ISO 12,800) additional noise is present in the image. Additional noise reduction can be engaged when the T1i is set for high ISO by using C.Fn 5.

This full ISO range (expanded or not) is only available in the Creative Zone exposure modes (see pages 140-148). In the Basic Zone modes (see pages 137-140), ISO is set automatically from 100-1600 and you cannot override it. There are two exceptions to the 100-1600 range:

- In portrait mode ♥ ISO is locked at 100 unless flash is used, then it is locked at 400.
- If flash is used with other Basic Zones, ISO is locked at 400 unless the camera determines that the image will be overexposed. If it will be overexposed, the ISO is adjusted to a lower setting. If an accessory flash is used in a bounce position, the ISO range reverts to 400-1600.

Note: Two Basic Zones won't use flash even if it is popped up manually: Sports ❄ and Flash Off ⚡. In these cases ISO is automatically set from 100-1600.

ISO speed can be set quickly from shot to shot in the Creative Zone. Since sensitivity to light is easily adjustable using a D-SLR, and since the Rebel T1i offers clean images with minimal noise at any standard setting, ISO is a control to use freely so you can rapidly adapt to changing light conditions.

High ISO settings can lead to noise (the digital equivalent of grain),in your pictures. Low ISO settings give the least

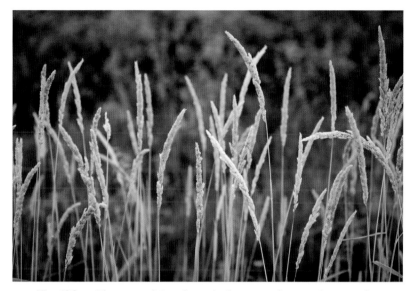

The ISO setting can determine whether your image shows noise (the digital equivalent of film grain) in darker areas. Lower ISO settings show almost no noise, and higher ISO settings show little to some noise, depending on your shooting environment and the amount of light.

amount of noise and the best color. Traditionally, film would increase in grain and decrease in sharpness with increased ISO. This is not entirely true with the Rebel T1i because its image is extremely clean. Noise is virtually nonexistent at ISO settings of less than 800. Some increase in noise may be noticed as settings of 800 or 1600 are used, but there will be little change in sharpness. Even the settings of 800 and 1600 offer very good results, but make sure you check the image on a computer to see if the noise is acceptable. This opens your digital photography to new possibilities for using slow lenses (lenses with smaller maximum lens openings, which are usually physically smaller as well) and in shooting with natural light.

Setting the ISO: To set the ISO speed, use the ISO button located on the top right shoulder of the camera, immediately behind ⌂. The ISO Speed menu displays on the LCD monitor and in the viewfinder. Use ▲▼ or ⌂ to select the sensitivity that you want. Once selected, press ⊛, ISO, or the shutter button. The selected ISO setting appears on the camera settings display on the LCD monitor.

The ISO settings occur in one-stop increments (100, 200, 400, 800, 1600, and 3200). Most of the time you will want to choose among several key ISO settings: 100 to capture detail in images of nature, landscape, and architecture; 400 when more speed is needed, such as handholding for portraits when shooting with a long lens; 800 and 1600 when you really need the extra speed under low-light conditions.

Auto ISO: You can also let the T1i decide which ISO to use. One of the options in the ISO Speed Menu is [AUTO]. When selected, the T1i chooses an ISO from 100 to 1600. When you use Flash ⚡ or Manual Exposure **M** modes, the ISO is set to 400. (In Basic Zone modes, Auto ISO operates under different rules; see page 137.) Auto ISO can be used in combination with Aperture Priority Autoexposure **Av** and Shutter Priority Autoexposure **Tv** modes (see page 141 and 145) to give you enhanced control of exposure settings. For example, if you want the highest shutter speed, set the mode to **Av**, open up the aperture to its widest setting and turn on Auto ISO. This guarantees that the T1i is set for the highest shutter speed for the amount of light in the scene.

Note: You can also set the ISO speed using the Quick Control screen. With the shooting settings displayed on the LCD monitor, press ⊛ and use ✧ to highlight the current ISO setting. Then use ⌂ to scroll through the ISO options, or you can press ⊛ to bring up the ISO options and then use ⌂ to make your selection. Next, tap the shutter release or press ⊛ to exit.

Metering

In order to produce the proper exposure, the camera's metering system has to evaluate the light. However, even today there is no light meter that produces a perfect exposure in every situation. Because different details of the subject reflect light in different amounts, the Rebel T1i's metering system has been designed with microprocessors and special sensors that give the system optimum flexibility and accuracy in determining exposure.

The camera offers four user-selectable methods of measuring light (metering modes): Evaluative ⊡ (linked to any desired AF point), Partial ⊡, Spot ⊡, and Center-weighted Average ⊏⊐. To select a metering mode, go to ◻⁝, use ▲▼ to highlight [Metering mode], and press ⊛. The Metering Mode menu displays on the LCD monitor. Scroll with ▲▼ to select the mode you want. Once selected, press ⊛ or the shutter button. The symbol or icon for the type of metering in use appears on the camera settings display on the LCD monitor.

Evaluative Metering ⊡: The Rebel T1i's Evaluative metering system divides the image area into 35 zones, "intelligently" compares them, and then uses advanced algorithms to determine exposure. The zones come from a grid of carefully designed metering areas that cover the frame, though there are fewer at the edges. Basically, the system evaluates and compares all of the metering zones across the image, noting things like the subject's position in the viewfinder (based on focus points and contrast), brightness of the subject compared to the rest of the image, backlighting, and much more.

The Rebel T1i's Evaluative metering system is linked to autofocus. The camera actually notes which autofocus point is active and emphasizes the corresponding metering zones in its evaluation of the overall exposure. If the system detects a significant difference between the main point of focus and the different areas that surround this point, the camera automatically applies exposure compensation. (It assumes the scene includes a backlit or spot-lit subject.) However, if the area around the focus point is very bright or dark, the metering can be thrown off and the camera may underexpose or overexpose the image. When your lens is set to manual focus, Evaluative metering uses the center autofocus point.

Note: With Evaluative metering, after autofocus has been achieved, exposure values are locked as long as the shutter button is partially depressed. However, meter readings cannot be locked in this manner if the lens is set for Manual focus. In those cases, use the AE lock button ✷, located on the back of the camera toward the upper right corner.

It is difficult to capture perfect exposures when shooting extremely dark or light subjects, subjects with unusual reflectance, or backlit subjects. Because the meter theoretically bases its analysis of light on an average gray scene, when subjects or the scene differ greatly from average gray, the meter tends to overexpose or underexpose them. Luckily, you can check exposure information in the viewfinder, or check the image itself—and its histogram—on the LCD monitor, and make adjustments as needed.

The main advantage of Evaluative metering over Partial, Spot, and Center-weighted Average metering is that the exposure is biased toward the active AF point rather than the center of the picture. Plus, Evaluative metering is the only metering mode that automatically applies exposure compensation based on comparative analysis of the scene.

Partial Metering ⊡**:** Partial metering covers about 9% of the frame, utilizing the exposure zones at the center of the viewfinder. It allows the photographer to selectively meter portions of a scene and compare the readings in order to select the right overall exposure. This can be an extremely accurate way of metering, but it requires some experience to do well. When you shoot with a telephoto lens, Partial metering acts like Spot metering.

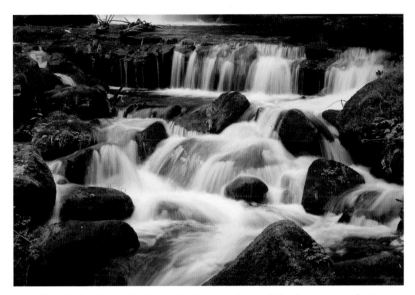

The Evaluative metering selection works well for images such as the one shown here; it takes an even reading from across the entire frame.

Spot Metering ⊡: Use this mode to further reduce the area covered for metering. The metering is weighted to the center area (about 4%) of the viewfinder. This can give you an extremely accurate meter reading of a single object in your scene.

Note: Just because spot metering only measures the center of the frame, it doesn't mean your subject has to stay in the center. Meter the subject from the center of the frame, use ✱ to lock exposure, and then reframe the composition (see page 149).

Center-Weighted Average Metering ⊏⊐: This method averages the readings taken across the entire scene. In computing the "average exposure", however, the camera puts extra emphasis on the reading taken from the center of the horizontal frame. Since most early traditional SLR cameras used this method exclusively, some photographers have used Center-weighted Average metering for such a long time that it is second nature and they prefer sticking with it. It can be very useful with scenes that change quickly around the subject.

One area in which to be careful with regard to exposure and this camera, is the viewfinder eyepiece. This may sound odd, yet if you shoot a long exposure on a tripod and do not have your eye to the eyepiece, there is a good possibility that your photo will be underexposed. The Rebel T1i's metering system is sensitive to light coming through an open eyepiece. To prevent this, Canon has included an eyepiece cover on the camera strap. It can be slipped over the viewfinder to block the opening in these conditions. You can quickly check the effect by watching the camera settings on the LCD monitor as you cover and uncover the eyepiece—you'll see how much the exposure can change. You'll need to set the [LCD auto off] function in ♥ to [Disable] (see page 69) to see the display while you cover the eyepiece.

Note: A faster method of setting metering mode is to use the Quick Control screen. With the shooting settings displayed on the LCD monitor, press ☜ and use ❖ to highlight the current metering method. Then use ⌂ to scroll through the metering options; or you can press ☜ to bring up the Meter mode screen and then use ⌂ to make your selection. Next, tap the shutter release or press ☜ to exit.

Judging Exposure

The LCD monitor allows you to get an idea of your photo's exposure—it's like using a Polaroid, although not as accurate. With a little practice, however, you can use this small image to evaluate your desired exposure. Recognize that because of the LCD monitor's calibration, size, and resolution, it only gives an indication of what you will actually see when the images are downloaded into your computer.

The Rebel T1i includes two features—Highlight alert and the Histogram—that give you a good indication of whether or not each exposure is correct. These features can be seen on the LCD monitor once an image is displayed there. Push DISP. repeatedly to cycle through a series of four displays: (1) Both the image and its exposure information; (2) The image and exposure, recording quality, and number of images; (3) A small image with Highlight alert, a histogram (brightness or RGB depending on the histogram setting in ⊡'), and extended image information; and (4) A small image with Highlight alert, both the brightness histogram and the RGB histogram, and reduced image information.

Highlight Alert

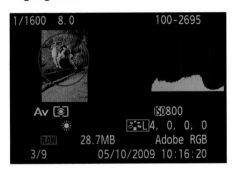

The highlight alert warns you of overexposure by flashing clipped areas. These bright areas in the image switch between white and black.

The camera's Highlight alert is very straightforward: Overexposed highlight areas blink on the small photo displayed next to the histogram. These areas have so much exposure that only white is recorded, no detail. Although it is helpful to immediately see what highlights are getting blown out, some photographers find the blinking a distraction. Blinking highlights are simply information, and not necessarily bad. Some scenes have less important areas that get washed out when the most important parts of the scene are exposed correctly. However, if you discover that significant areas of your subject are blinking, the image is likely overexposed and you need to reduce exposure in some way.

The Histogram

The Rebel T1i's histogram, though small, is an extremely important tool. It is the graph that appears on the LCD monitor next to the image when selected with DISP. during review or playback. The T1i can display two different kinds of histograms: Brightness and RGB. The Brightness histogram allows you to judge the overall exposure of the image, while the RGB histogram focuses in on the individual color channels.

The brightness histogram allows you to evaluate exposure in the field. There is no perfect histogram, but it is a good practice to avoid large peaks at the far left and far right of the graph.

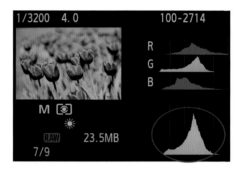

Brightness Histogram: The horizontal axis of the histogram represents the level of brightness—dark areas are at the left, bright areas are at the right. The vertical axis indicates the pixel quantity of the different levels of brightness. If the graph rises as a slope from the bottom left corner of the histogram and then descends towards the bottom right corner, all the tones of the scene are captured.

Consider the graph from left to right (dark to bright). If the graph starts too high on either end, i.e., so the "slope" looks like it is abruptly cut off at either side, then the exposure data is also cut off or "clipped" at the ends because the sensor is incapable of handling the areas darker or brighter than those points. An example would be a dark, shadowed subject on a bright, sunny day.

Or, the histogram may be weighted towards either the dark or bright side of the graph (wider, higher "hills" appear on one side or the other). This is okay if the scene is naturally dark or bright, but if it is not, detail may be lost. However, be careful of dark scenes that have all the data in the left half of the histogram. Such underexposure tends to overemphasize any sensor noise that might be present. You are better off increasing the exposure, even if the LCD image looks bright enough. You can always darken the image in the computer, which will not affect grain; yet lightening a very dark image usually has an adverse effect and results in added noise.

If highlights are important, be sure that the slope on the right reaches the bottom of the graph before it hits the right axis. If darker areas are important, be sure the slope on the left reaches the bottom before it hits the left axis. You really don't have to remember which side is dark or light at first. If you notice an unbalanced graph, just give the scene a change of exposure and notice which way the histogram changes. This is a good way to learn to read the histogram.

If the scene is low in contrast, the histogram appears as a rather narrow hill in the middle of the graph, leaving gaps with no data toward both the left and right axes. To help this situation, check the Rebel T1i's Picture Styles (see page 93). Boosting contrast expands the histogram—you can create a custom setting with contrast change and tonal curve adjustments that consistently addresses such a situation. This can mean better information is captured—it is spread out more evenly across the tones—before bringing the image into your computer to use image-processing software. You could also experiment with C.Fn 7, Auto Lighting Optimizer (see page 77). Or, you could use RAW, since results are best in RAW when the data has been stretched to make better use of the tonal range from black to white.

Note: When shooting RAW the effects of the Auto Lighting Optimizer will only be apparent if the RAW file is processed through Canon's Digital Photo Professional software.

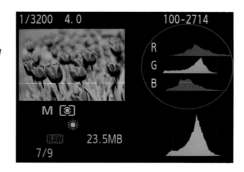

The RGB histogram is not quite as useful as the brightness histogram, but it is useful to see if you have overexposed one of the color channels.

RGB Histogram: When you use the RGB histogram, you can check to see if any individual color channels are over-saturated. Similar to the Brightness histogram, the horizontal scale represents each color channel's brightness level—if more pixels are to the left, the color is less prominent and darker; to the right, the color is brighter and denser. If the histogram shows an abrupt cut-off on either end of the histogram, your color information is either missing or over-saturated. In short, by checking the RGB histogram, you can evaluate the color saturation and white balance effect.

Shooting Modes

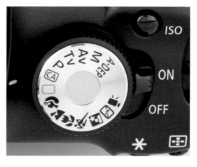

The mode dial, on the top right of the T1i, controls which shooting mode the T1i is in. The settings are arrange into two groups or zones.

The Rebel T1i offers 13 still shooting modes and one movie mode divided into two groups: the Basic Zone and the Creative Zone. In the Basic Zone, the primary benefit is that the camera can be matched quickly to conditions or to a subject. Fast and easy to manage, the modes in the Basic Zone permit the camera to predetermine a number of settings. In some of these modes, all the controls are set by the camera and cannot be adjusted by the photographer.

Hint: It helps to understand that Basic Zones are shooting modes where the camera is responsible for setting up most of the camera settings. Creative Zones, on the other hand, are "exposure modes" where the camera only pays attention to the exposure setting, specifically shutter speed, aperture, and sometimes ISO speed. You have to do the rest.

All shooting modes, including the Basic Zone modes, are selected by using the Mode dial ⊙ located on the top right of the camera. Simply rotate the dial to the icon you wish to use. Basic Zone modes are identified by a picture icon; Creative Zone modes are selected with the letter icons.

Note: When you are in any of the Basic Zone modes, the ⬛, ⬛, and ⬛ menus, as well as various other menu items, are not accessible. In addition, all Basic Zones except Full Auto ◻ require you to select the file size and compression options. The T1i will set color space to sRGB, white balance to ⬛⬛, metering to ⬛, and ISO to Auto ISO. In Basic Zones these settings cannot be changed.

Basic Zone Shooting Modes

Full Auto ◻: The green rectangle selects Full Auto, which is used for completely automatic shooting. This mode essentially converts the Rebel T1i into a point-and-shoot camera—a very sophisticated point-and-shoot! The camera chooses everything; you cannot adjust any controls except file quality/size and drive mode. This is really designed for the beginning photographer who hasn't learned the T1i yet or for times when you hand the camera to someone to take a picture of you. That way they can't mess up settings. The Picture Style is Standard ⬛⬛ for crisp, vivid images; the white balance is set for ⬛⬛; ISO speed is Auto; and focus mode is set for **AI FOCUS**. The flash will pop up and fire if needed.

Note: Keep in mind that manual focus can be engaged on the lens and will override any focus setting in any shooting mode.

Creative Auto ⒸⒶ:This mode is similar to ▢ but with the opportunity to make more adjustments. You can use the Quick Control screen to turn on/off flash and to adjust Background, Exposure, Picture Style, file size/format and drive mode.

The "Background" and "Exposure" settings are unique to ⒸⒶ. The Background setting is another way of adjusting depth-of-field. You can make adjustments from "Blurred" to "Sharp". What this really does is adjust the aperture setting (f-stop) of the camera.

The Exposure setting operates the same way as exposure compensation (page 150). The center position on the range is no exposure compensation, the two positions to the right represent +2/3 and +1 1/3 stops of over-exposure adjustment and the two positions to the left indicate -2/3 and -1 1/3 stops of under-exposure.

The Picture Style setting is a little more limited than normal, offering just Standard ⬛S, Portrait ⬛P, Landscape ⬛L and Monochrome ⬛M. You can't make any further adjustments to the Picture Style parameters like you can in non-automatic modes. In fact, if you make adjustments to Picture Styles before you enter ⒸⒶ mode, you won't see those adjustments to the Picture Styles--they will be set to their default values.

For drive mode, ⒸⒶ allows you to select single shot ▢, continuous shooting ⊒, in addition to ⚫ and ⚫₂.

Portrait ☙: If you like to shoot portraits, this setting is for you. It makes adjustment choices that favor people photography. The drive is set to Continuous ⊒ so you can quickly shoot changing gestures and expressions (but you can change it to ⚫ or ⚫c), while the AF mode is set to **ONE SHOT** so you can lock focus with a slight pressing of the shutter

138

release. The meter favors wider f/stops (those with smaller numbers) because this limits depth of field, offering backgrounds that are softer and therefore contrast with the sharper focus of the subject. A wider f/stop also results in faster shutter speeds, producing sharper handheld images. Picture Style is set to Portrait ≋ for softer skin tones (see page 94). The flash will fire if needed.

Landscape ▲: When shooting landscape photography, it is important to lock focus on one shot at a time, so Landscape mode uses **ONE SHOT** AF and ☐ Drive mode (but you can change it to ⚡ or ⚡c). The meter favors small f/stops for more depth of field (often important for scenic shots). Picture Style is set to Landscape ≋ for vivid greens and blues. The flash does not fire.

Close-up ❀: This mode also uses **ONE SHOT** AF and ☐ Drive mode (but ⚡ and ⚡c are also available). It favors wider f/stops for faster shutter speeds, giving better sharpness with a handheld camera and far less depth of field in order to set off a sharp subject against a softer background. Picture Style is set to Standard ≋. The flash fires if needed.

Sports ⚡: Designed for action and fast shutter speeds to stop the action of your subject, this uses **AI SERVO** AF and ⚟ Drive mode (but you can change drive mode to ⚡ or ⚡c), both of which allow continuous shooting as action evolves in front of you. In addition, the beep for AF confirmation is softer than other modes. Picture Style is ≋. The flash does not fire.

Night Portrait ❂: Despite its name, this setting is not limited to nighttime use. It is very useful, even for advanced photographers, to balance flash with low-light conditions. This setting uses flash to illuminate the subject (which may or may not be a portrait), as well as an exposure setting (shutter speed, ISO and aperture) to balance the background, bringing in the subject's detail. The latter exposure, called the ambient light exposure, can have a very slow shutter speed and may result in a blurry background, so you may need a tripod if that is not the effect you are going for. The Picture Style is ⬛⬛⬛. Like most of the Basic Zone modes, Night Portrait defaults to ☐ Drive mode but can be switched to ⟲ᵢ or ⟲c.

Flash Off ⚡: This mode provides a quick and easy setting that prevents the flash from firing. Think of this mode as operating the same as ☐ except the flash will never fire. In fact, you can even pop up the flash using the ⚡ button. If the flash is popped before you enter ⚡ it still won't fire. This is the mode to use when museums and other sensitive locations ask that there be no flash photography.

Creative Zone Shooting Modes

The Creative Zone modes are appropriately named. They offer more control over camera adjustments and thus encourage a more creative approach to photography. The disadvantage is that there are many possible adjustments, which can be confusing at worst, and time consuming at best. Again, all modes in the Creative Zone are engaged by turning ◎ to the desired designation, one of the letter icons. Many of the setting adjustments—displayed on the LCD monitor and viewfinder—are made by turning the Main dial ⛯ (top right shoulder of camera).

Remember that when shooting in the "zone" (Creative Zone), settings such as white balance, file type (RAW or JPEG), metering method, focus method, Picture Style, ISO, and Drive mode need to be set manually—the camera is only concerned about exposure.

Program AE Mode P: In Program AE (autoexposure) mode, the camera chooses the shutter speed and aperture combination. This gives the photographer less direct control over the exposure because no matter how apt, the settings are chosen arbitrarily (by the camera, not by you). However, you can shift the "program" by changing either the selected aperture or shutter speed, and the system compensates to maintain the same exposure value. To shift the program, simply press the shutter button halfway—this turns on the camera's built-in light meter, then turn ⛯ until the desired shutter speed or aperture value (respectively) is displayed on the LCD monitor or viewfinder.

Hint: Think of aperture and shutter speed like two sides of a balance scale that measures light. If you increase the amount of light let in by the aperture the camera will shorten the length of time that the shutter is open (shutter speed).

Note: Program shift only works for one exposure at a time, making it useful for quick-and-easy shooting while retaining some control over camera settings.

The flash will not pop up automatically in **P** mode when light levels are low. You must manually engage the flash by pressing the ⚡ button on the left side of the camera above the lens release button. Also, program shift does not work with flash.

P selects shutter speed and aperture values steplessly. This means that any shutter speed or aperture within the range of the camera and lens is selected, not just those that are the standard full steps, such as 1/250 second or f/16. This is common for most SLRs (both film and digital) and allows for extremely precise exposure accuracy, thanks to the lens' electromagnetically controlled diaphragm and the camera's electronically timed shutter.

Shutter-Priority AE Mode Tv: Tv stands for "time value". In this mode you set the shutter speed (using 🔄) and the camera sets the aperture. If you want a particular shutter speed for artistic reasons—perhaps a high speed to stop action or a slow speed for a blur effect—this is the setting to use. In this mode, even if the light varies, the shutter speed does not. The camera keeps up with changing light by adjusting the aperture automatically. If the aperture indicated in the viewfinder or the LCD monitor is consistently lit (not blinking), the T1i has picked a useable aperture. If the maximum aperture (lowest number) blinks, it means the photo will be underexposed. Select a slower shutter speed by turning 🔄 until the aperture indicator stops blinking. You can also remedy this by increasing the ISO setting. If the minimum aperture (highest number)

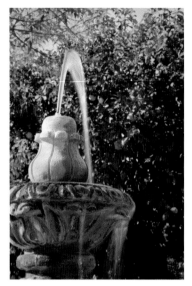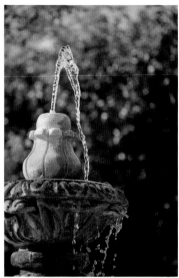

Shutter speed can determine how quickly-moving subjects are rendered in your image. A slower shutter speed gives the water a feeling of motion (left), and a faster shutter speed freezes the water (right). When the shutter speed was adjusted it affected aperture. Notice how the depth of field is also different between the two shots.

blinks, this indicates overexposure. In this case, you should set a faster shutter speed until the blinking stops, or choose a lower ISO setting.

The Rebel T1i offers a choice of speeds, from 1/4000 second up to 30 seconds in 1/3-stop increments (1/2-stop increments with C.Fn 1; see page 74), plus Bulb setting **BULB**. For flash exposures, the camera syncs at 1/200 second or slower (which is important to know since slower shutter speeds can be used to pick up ambient or existing light in a dimly-lit scene).

Let's examine these shutter speeds by designating them "fast", "moderate", and "slow". (These divisions are arbitrarily chosen, so speeds at either end of a division can really be designated into the groups on either side of it.)

Fast shutter speeds are 1/500–1/4000 second. It wasn't all that long ago that most film cameras could only reach 1/1000 second, so having this range of high speeds on a digital SLR is quite remarkable. The obvious reason to choose these speeds is to stop action. The more the action increases in pace, or the closer it crosses directly in front of you, the higher the speed you need. As mentioned previously, the neat thing about a digital camera is that you can check your results immediately on the LCD monitor to see if the shutter speed has, in fact, frozen the action.

At these fast speeds, camera movement during exposure is rarely significant unless you try to handhold a super telephoto lens of 600mm (not recommended!). This means, with proper handholding technique, you can shoot using most normal focal lengths (from wide-angle to telephoto up to about 300mm) without blur resulting from camera movement.

Besides stopping action, high shutter speeds allow you to use your lens at its widest openings (such as f/2.8 or f/4) for selective focus effects (shallow depth of field). This is a useful technique. In bright sun, for example, you might have an exposure of 1/200 second at f/16 with an ISO setting of 200. You can get to f/2.8 by increasing your speed by five whole steps of exposure, to approximately 1/4000 second.

Note: Remember the balance between shutter speed and aperture. In **Tv** the camera automatically selects the aperture when you set the shutter speed. Try this yourself. Go outside and use 🔄 to set the shutter to 1/200. Now, look in the viewfinder, ignore the shutter speed and just watch the aperture. Keep rotating 🔄 until the aperture is at the widest setting that the lens will allow. Now look and see how short the shutter speed has become.

Moderate shutter speeds (1/60-1/250 second) work for most subjects and allow a reasonable range of f/stops to be used. They are the real workhorse shutter speeds, as long as there's no fast action. You have to be careful when handholding cameras at the lower end of this range—especially with telephoto lenses—or you may notice blur in your pictures from camera movement during the exposure. Many photographers find that they cannot handhold a camera with moderate focal lengths (50-150mm) at shutter speeds less than 1/125 second without some degradation of the image due to camera movement. You can double-check your technique by taking a photograph of a scene while handholding the camera and then comparing it to the same scene shot using a tripod. Be sure to magnify the image to check for image blur caused by camera motion. (Even better, check it on the computer.)

Note: Lenses with image stabilization (Canon lenses with this feature are labeled IS) can help you shoot hand held with slower shutter speeds but they might only give you an extra stop.

Slow shutter speeds (1/60 second or slower) require something to stabilize the camera. Some photographers may discover they can handhold a camera and shoot relatively sharp images at the high end of this range, but most cannot get optimal sharpness from their lenses at these speeds without a tripod or another stabilizing mount. Slow shutter speeds are used mainly for low-light conditions and to allow the use of smaller f/stops (higher f/numbers—increasing depth of field) under all conditions.

A fun use of very slow shutter speeds (1/8–1/2 second) is to photograph movement, such as a waterfall or runners, or to move the camera during exposure, such as panning it across a scene. The effects are quite unpredictable, but again, image review using the LCD monitor helps. You can try different shutter speeds and see what your images look like. This is helpful when you try to choose a slow speed appropriate for the subject because each speed blurs action differently.

You can set slow shutter speeds (up to 30 seconds) for special purposes, such as capturing fireworks or moonlit landscapes. Canon has engineered the sensor and its accompanying circuits to minimize noise (a common problem of long exposures with digital cameras) and the Rebel T1i offers remarkable results with these exposures. C.Fn 4 can be used to reduce noise even more (see page 75).

In contrast to long exposures using film, long digital exposures are not susceptible to reciprocity. The reciprocity effect comes with film because as exposures lengthen beyond approximately one second (depending on the film), the sensitivity of the film declines, resulting in the need to increase exposure to compensate. A metered 30-second film exposure might actually require double or triple that time to achieve the effect that is desired. Digital cameras do not have this problem. A metered exposure of 30 seconds is all that is actually needed.

Aperture-Priority AE Mode Av: In **Av** (aperture value) mode, you set the aperture (the f/stop or lens opening) and the camera selects the appropriate shutter speed for a proper exposure. This is probably the most popular automatic exposure setting among professional photographers.

One of the most common reasons to use **Av** mode is to control depth of field (the distance in front of and behind a specific plane of focus that is acceptably sharp). While the f/stop, or aperture, affects the amount of light entering the camera, it also has a direct effect on depth of field. A small lens opening (higher f/number) such as f/11 or f/16 increases the depth of field in the photograph, bringing objects in the distance into sharper focus when the lens is focused appropriately. Higher f/numbers are great for landscape photography.

A wide lens opening with low f/numbers such as f/2.8 or f/4 decreases the depth of field. These lower f/numbers work well when you want to take a photo of a sharp subject that creates a contrast with a soft, out-of-focus background. If the shutter speed blinks in the viewfinder (or on the LCD monitor), it means the shutter speed the camera wants to use is not available on the camera. In other words, good exposure is not possible at that aperture, so determine whether you need to change the aperture to limit light (change it to f/8 or f/11, for example) or to decrease the ISO speed setting to make the T1i less sensitive to light.

You can see the effect of the aperture setting on the depth-of-field by pushing the camera's Depth-of-field preview button, located on front of the camera below the lens release button. This stops the lens down to the taking aperture and reveals sharpness in the resulting darkened viewfinder (the lens otherwise remains wide-open until the next picture is taken). Using Depth-of-field preview takes some practice due to the darkened viewfinder, but changes in focus can be seen if you look hard enough. You can also check focus in the LCD monitor after the shot (magnify as needed).

Note: When you press the Depth-of-field preview button you are only concerned about evaluating depth of field; don't worry about how dark things look.

This sounds counterintuitive, but a sports or wildlife photographer might choose **Av** mode in order to stop action rather than to capture depth of field. To accomplish this, he or she selects a wide lens opening—perhaps f/2.8 or f/4—to let in the maximum amount of light. The camera automatically selects the fastest shutter speed possible for the conditions. Compare this with **Tv** mode. There you can set a fast shutter speed, but the camera still may not be able to expose correctly if the light drops and the selected shutter speed requires an opening larger than the particular lens can provide. (The aperture value blinks in the viewfinder if this is the case.) As a result, photographers typically select **Tv** only when they have to use a specific shutter speed. Otherwise they use **Av** to both control depth of field and to gain the fastest possible shutter speed for the circumstances.

Note: One exception to using **Av** to get a fast shutter speed is to instead use **Tv** but then use Auto ISO. For example, if you are shooting a certain sporting event and you discover that you need 1/500, you could set that while in **Tv** and then, if the aperture was as the end of its range (widest open that the lens will go), the Auto ISO function will kick up the camera's sensitivity.

146

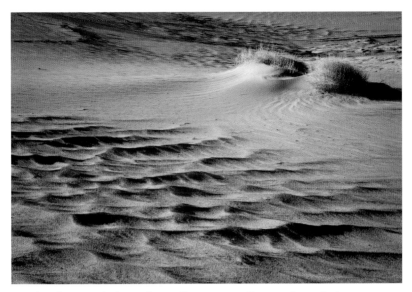

Landscape photographers often use smaller apertures to increase the depth of field in an image, as shown in the above example.

Automatic Depth-of-Field AE A-DEP: This is a unique exposure mode that Canon has used on a number of EOS SLRs (both film and digital) over the years. **A-DEP** simplifies the selection of an f/stop to ensure maximum depth of field for a subject. The camera actually checks focus, comparing all nine AF points to determine the distance between the closest and farthest points in the scene. The camera then picks an aperture to cover that distance and the appropriate shutter speed. You cannot control either yourself. It also sets the focus distance. If the camera cannot get an aperture to match the depth of field needed to cover the near and far points, the aperture blinks. You can check what the depth of field looks like by pressing the Depth-of-field preview button. You must use AF (autofocus) on the lens; MF (Manual Focus) makes the camera act like **P** is set. **A-DEP** does not work with flash. If you turn on the flash the camera again acts like **P** is set.

Manual Exposure Mode: This is the one setting in the Creative Zone that is not an auto exposure mode. This option is important for photographers who are used to working in full manual and for anyone who faces certain tricky situations. (However, since this camera is designed to give exceptional automatic exposures, I recommend that everyone try the automatic settings at times to see what they can do). In **M**, you set both the shutter speed (using 🖾) and aperture (hold down the Av☒ button located on back of the camera near the upper right corner of the LCD, then turn the 🖾 dial).

You can use the camera's exposure metering systems to guide you through manual exposure settings. The current exposure is visible on the scale at the bottom of the viewfinder information display. "Correct" exposure is at the mid-point, and you can see how much the exposure settings vary from that point by observing the scale. The scale shows up to two f/stops over or under the mid-point, allowing you to quickly compensate for bright or dark subjects (especially when using Partial ⊡ metering). If the pointer on the scale blinks, the exposure is off the scale. Of course, you can also use a hand-held meter.

The following examples of complex metering conditions might require you to use **M** mode: Panoramic shooting (you need a consistent exposure across the multiple shots taken, and the only way to ensure that is with **M**—white balance should be one of the presets and not **AWB**); lighting conditions that change rapidly around a subject with consistent light (a theatrical stage, for example); close-up photography where the subject is in one light but slight movement of the camera dramatically changes the light behind it; and any conditions where you need a consistent exposure through varied lighting conditions.

Bulb Exposure BULB: This setting is not on the ◎, but is only found when the camera is set to **M**. It is an option following [30 seconds] when you scroll through shutter speeds. This mode allows you to control long exposures because the shutter stays open as long as you keep the shutter button depressed. Let go, and the shutter closes. A dedicated remote switch, such as the Canon RS-60E3, is helpful for these long exposures. It allows you to keep the shutter open without touching the camera (which can cause movement). It attaches to the camera's remote terminal (on the left side). You can use the RC-1 or RC-5 wireless remote switches for bulb exposures, as well.

When you use **BULB**, the camera shows the elapsed time (in seconds) for your exposure as long as you keep the shutter release or remote switch depressed. This can be quite helpful in knowing your exposure. At this point in digital camera technology, exposures beyond a few minutes start to have problems in the form of excessive noise. Still, the Rebel T1i allows longer exposures than most cameras of this type. It is a good idea to use C.Fn 4, Long exposure noise reduction, to apply added in-camera noise reduction (see page 75). Remember that long exposure noise reduction doubles the apparent exposure time, so make sure you have enough battery power.

AE Lock ✳

AE lock is a very useful tool in the autoexposure modes. Under normal operation, the camera continually updates exposure either as you move the camera across the scene or as the subject moves. This can be a problem if the light across the area is inconsistent yet remains constant on the subject. In this case, you want to lock the exposure on the subject. ✳ is also helpful when a scene is mostly in one light, yet your subject is in another. In that circumstance, try to find a spot nearby that has the same light as your subject, point the camera at it and lock exposure, then move the camera back to the original composition. (If you have a zoom lens mounted you could zoom in to a particular area of the scene, as well.)

AE lock on the Rebel T1i is similar to that used for most EOS cameras. The ✳ button is located on the back of the camera to the upper right, easily accessed with your thumb. Aim the camera where necessary for the proper exposure,

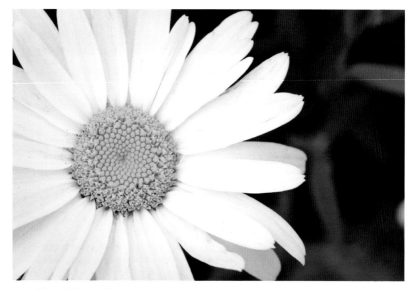

If a white subject fills the frame, such as shown here, the camera might meter to underexpose the image. Use the exposure compensation feature to determine the exposure that best suits your subject.

then push ✱. The exposure is locked or secured, and it won't change, even if you move the camera. ✱ appears in the viewfinder on the left of the information display until the lock is released.

The exposure will stay locked until the camera's metering system shuts down—about 4 seconds. You can tell that the metering system has shut down when the information display turns off in the viewfinder. If you want to keep the exposure locked longer—even through multiple shots—press and hold ✱. The meter stays on and the exposure stays locked until about 4 seconds after you let go.

Exposure Compensation Av🔲
The existence of a feature for exposure compensation, along with the ability to review images in the LCD monitor, means you can quickly override exposures without using **M**

mode. Exposure compensation cannot be used in **M** mode; however, it makes the **P**, **Tv**, **Av**, and **A-DEP** modes much more versatile. Compensation is added (for brighter exposure) or subtracted (for darker exposure) in f/stop increments of 1/3 for up to +/- 2 stops (1/2-stop increments with C. Fn 1; see page 74).

To use the exposure compensation feature, start by pressing the shutter button halfway to turn on the metering system. Then press and hold Av⊠ (on back of the camera near the upper right corner of the LCD monitor). Rotate ⌂ to change the compensation amount. The exact exposure compensation appears on the scale at the bottom of the viewfinder information display, as well as on the LCD monitor.

You can also adjust exposure compensation without turning on the metering system by just viewing the camera settings on the LCD monitor while pressing Av⊠ and turning ⌂. The Quick Control Screen is another way to adjust exposure compensation.

It is important to remember that once you set your exposure compensation control, it stays set even if you shut off the camera. Check your exposure setting as a regular habit (by looking at the bottom scale in the viewfinder information display) when you turn on your camera to be sure the compensation is not inadvertently set for a scene that doesn't need it. Turn exposure compensation off (set it to zero) by holding Av⊠ and turning ⌂ to set the scale in the LCD monitor or viewfinder back to zero.

With experience, you may find that you use exposure compensation routinely with certain subjects. Since the meter wants to increase exposure on dark subjects and decrease exposure on light subjects to make them closer to middle gray, exposure compensation may be necessary. For example, say you are photographing a grade school football game with the sun behind the players. The camera wants to underexpose in reaction to the bright sunlight, but the shaded sides of the players' bodies may be too dark. So you add exposure with the exposure compensation feature. Or maybe the game is in front of densely shaded bleachers. In this case the players would be overexposed because the camera wants to react to the darkness. Here, you subtract exposure. In both cases, the camera consistently maintains the exposure you have selected until you readjust the exposure settings.

The LCD monitor can come in handy when you experiment with exposure compensation. Take a test shot, and then check the photo and its histogram. If it looks good, go with it. If the scene is too bright, subtract exposure; if it's too dark, add it. Again, remember that if you want to return to making exposures without using compensation, you must move the setting back to zero!

Auto Exposure Bracketing (AEB)

The Rebel T1i offers another way to apply exposure compensation: The Auto Exposure Bracketing control (AEB). AEB tells the camera to make three consecutive exposures that are different: (1) A standard exposure or center shot; (2) An image with less exposure; and (3) One with more exposure. These two shots are said to "bracket" the "normal" exposure.

The difference between exposures can be set up to +/- 2 stops in 1/3-stop increments. (C.Fn 1 allows you to change this to 1/2-stop increments—see page 74.) The "center" shot could already have an exposure compensation set. While using AEB, the Rebel T1i changes the shutter speed in **Av** mode and aperture in **Tv** mode.

Note: If the T1i is in Auto ISO mode and AEB needs to use an exposure setting beyond the range of the camera, the ISO speed will be adjusted. So you could pick a shutter speed where the aperture doesn't change through the bracketed shots, but the ISO speed does.

AEB is set through $\Box$. Scroll to [Expo.comp./AEB] and press ⑯. The submenu gives you to the ability to adjust both exposure compensation and bracketing. Use ◀▶ to adjust compensation on the center shot between the under and over exposed shots, then use 🔆 to set the bracketing amount. The short outer lines show the exposure setting for under and over shots and the long line is the "center" exposure. Make sure you press ⑤ to accept the change.

Note: If C.Fn 1 is set for 1/2-stop increments (see page 74), the bracket amount will use 1/2-stop increments.

Hint: Put the Quick Control Screen to work for you. It is the quickest way to AEB. See page 152 to learn more.

When in ☐ Drive mode, you must press the shutter button for each of the three shots. As you shoot, a marker appears on the exposure scale at the bottom of the viewfinder information display. This marker indicates which exposure is being used with the AEB sequence. In 🔁 mode, the camera takes the three shots and stops. When you use ⏱ and ⏱2, all three shots are taken. With ⏱c, each of the shots at the end of the countdown is bracketed. This means if you set ⏱c for six, you end up with 18 images; however, the camera buffer fills up quickly, so after the first couple shots are taken, the T1i waits until the images in the buffer are written to the memory card before the remaining shots are taken.

Note: When set to AEB, the camera continues to take three different exposures in a row until you reset the control to zero, turn the camera off, change lenses, or replace the SD card or battery.

AEB can help ensure that you get the best possible image files for later adjustment using image-processing software. A dark original file always has the potential for increased noise as it is adjusted, and a light image may lose important detail in the highlights. AEB can help you to determine the best exposure for the situation. You won't use it all the time, but it can be very useful when the light in the scene varies in contrast or is complex in its dark and light values.

AEB is also important for a special digital editing technique that allows you to put multiple exposures together into one master to gain more tonal range from a scene. You can take the well-exposed highlights of one exposure and combine them with the better-detailed shadows of another. (This works best with 1/2-stop bracketing.) If you carefully shot the exposures with your camera on a tripod, they will line up exactly so that when you put the images on top of one another as layers using image-processing software, the different exposures are easy to combine. (You may even want to set the camera to ⊒⌿—in this mode it takes the three photos for the AEB sequence and then stops.)

Note: This technique is sometimes referred to as HDR photography—high dynamic range. There are software applications that can merge these files together and help you choose which parts of which image to use. In order for HDR to be successful, a tripod is a necessity. You'll also need to shoot with aperture priority (so depth of field doesn't change), preset white balance (not **AWB**, so color doesn't change), and manual focus or a locked focus (so that focus doesn't change). HDR works best with images that have little or no movement.

You can combine exposure compensation with AEB to handle a variety of difficult situations. But remember, while AEB resets when you turn off the camera, exposure compensation does not.

Difficult exposures require patience when photographing. The butterfly was lit by a small beam of sunlight that snuck through the forest canopy, yet the rest of the foliage was very shady. ⊳

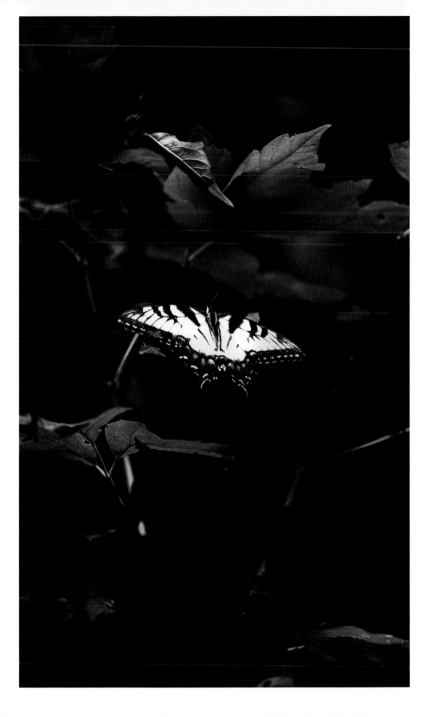

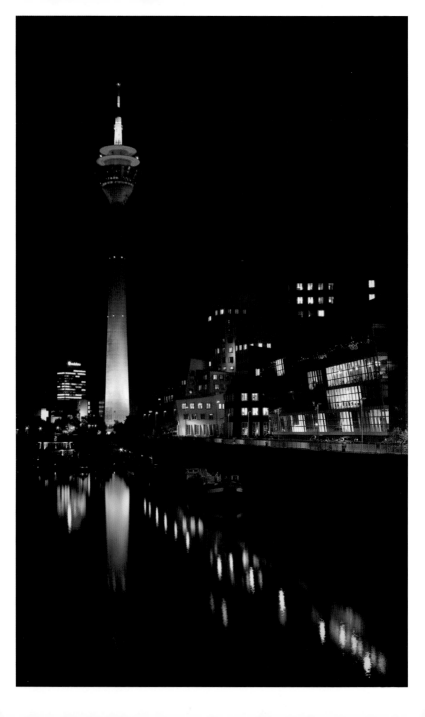

Live View Shooting
and Movie Mode

As noted in previous chapters, the LCD monitor is invaluable in reviewing your shots and making menu selections. But there's more. It is also essential in Live View shooting of stills and in Movie recording.

Previously, people stepping up from a point-and-shoot camera to a D-SLR kept asking, "Why can't I see the image on the LCD before I take the shot? My little camera that is one fourth of the price can do it!" Live View has changed all that.

Canon was one of the first manufacturers to offer Live View shooting in a D-SLR. This technology, which allows you to see an image on the LCD monitor before you shoot, allows you to frame shots when it is difficult to look through the viewfinder. It also allows you to check exposure, composition, color, and focus on a computer display: when you connect the T1i to a computer and run the Canon-provided software, you can view images live on the computer.

Note: Since Live View shooting and Movie recording share the same technology and some of the same camera settings, this chapter deals with both in tandem. But keep in mind when I refer to Live View shooting I am talking about capturing stills; Movie recording refers to operation of the T1i when the Mode Dial ◎ is set for '🎥.

🔁 *Live View shooting is available with the Rebel T1i, and can be a great tool when shooting long exposures from a tripod where you might not want to hold the camera to your face for the entire exposure. It frees you to move away from the camera and still see the composition.*

To enable Live View shooting, go to 🔧, scroll to highlight [Live View function settings], and press ⊛. Make sure [Live View shoot.] is highlighted in the subsequent menu screen, again press ⊛. Then use ▲▼ to highlight [Enable] and press ⊛ to confirm the setting. Once Live View shooting is enabled, press the 🗗 button at any time to turn it on.

To use Movie mode, rotate ◯ to 🎬. Movie mode does not require [Live View shoot.] to be enabled.

Live View and Movie Menus

The movie menu tab will only be present when the mode dial is in movie mode.

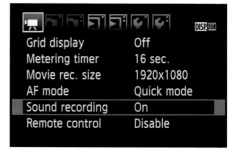

When the T1i is set for 🎬, an additional main menu tab, 🎬, is added to the left of 🗗. This menu is nearly identical to the Live View function settings submenu in 🔧.

Grid 1 is a useful tool for composing your scene according to the rule of thirds.

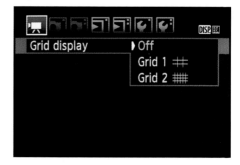

Grid display: Grids can be used to assist in leveling the camera and for help in composition. Grids are only displayed on the LCD monitor and are not embedded in the image.

Grid 1 looks like a tic-tac-toe game board and is useful as a guide for rule-of-thirds shooting. The rule of thirds divides the frame into nine areas, based on three equal horizontal spaces and three vertical spaces. You should place the main focus of your scene at one of the four intersections of the grid. Not all pictures have to follow the rule of thirds; it is just a starting point. The grid also reminds you not to put horizons smack dab in the middle of the frame.

Grid 2 is a denser grid of five vertical lines and three horizontal lines. This is a good tool when you need to make sure that the T1i is level and square to the scene you are photographing. For example, you might use it when you photograph a building.

Metering timer: Live View shooting often differs from non-Live View shooting. The camera might be tethered (or wirelessly connected) to a computer; the camera may be powered via the AC adaptor; or it might be used in a studio, where images are evaluated for longer periods of time. The T1i offers an extended AE lock timer when you shoot with Live View. The metering timer ranges from 4 seconds to 30 minutes, so you can now hold an exposure setting for half an hour, compared to the 4 seconds that occurs with non-Live View shooting.

AF mode: You can select from three different focusing methods: AF Quick, AF Live, and AF ⚘. You can also use the Live View Quick Control screen to set the AF method.

Note: Although the Live View and Movie mode menus appear in two different places, they share the same settings. In other words, if you set the metering timer for 1 minute in Live View it will be 1 minute in the Movie mode menu, as well.

In Movie mode there are some additional menu options:

Both 1920x1080 and 1280x720 are standard high definition resolutions, but 1920x1080 only records at 20 frames per second rather than the normal standard of 30 frames per second.

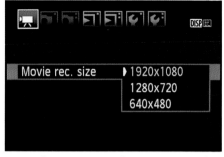

Movie rec. size: There are three options for movie resolution. Two of them are high definition (1920x1080 and 1280x720) and one is standard definition (640x480). See page 174 to learn more about video resolution.

The microphone is built-in to the T1i. Make sure that you don't cover the microphone holes when holding the camera.

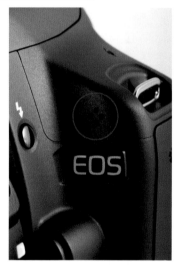

Sound recording: You can enable sound recording with this option. The audio is recorded with the built-in microphone on the front of the T1i (the four holes above the EOS logo). The audio is mono. Since the mic is built into the body of the camera it picks up any handling noise when you adjust the lens or press any button.

Remote control: By enabling this option you can use the wireless remotes (RC-1 or RC-5) to start the movie recording. If you are using the RC-1 wireless remote control for movie recording and you set the timing delay on the remote to 2, the T1i starts recording. If the delay is set to immediate, a still photo is taken.

Restrictions in Live View and Movie Mode

There are some limitations using Live View shooting. First, it can only be used when the camera is in one of the Creative Zone modes. In addition, the metering will always be set to ▣, AF operates differently and **A-DEP** behaves like **P**. Finally, Custom Function (C.Fn) 11 is automatically set to option [0] (see page 79).

Note: Live View shooting and Movie mode use a lot of power; make sure you have fully charged batteries on hand at all times. The T1i is good for about 190 shots using Live View and for 170 shots when flash is also used half the time. When recording movies the batteries last about 1 hour and 10 minutes. (These figures assume a temperature of 73°F/23°C.)

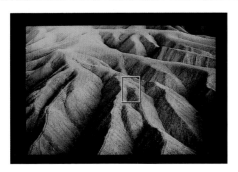

This is the basic Live View display mode, which just shows the AF point(s).

You can cycle through four display modes (three in movie mode) by pressing **DISP.**. The first display is just the image with the AF point. The second adds a status display at the bottom of the LCD showing exposure information (shutter speed and aperture when the meter is on), an exposure level indicator (including compensation and bracketing indicators if engaged), flash exposure compensation, shots remaining, ISO speed, highlight tone priority indicator, and battery level. In Movie mode the status display is similar except there is no flash exposure compensation and the shutter speed and aperture only represent the exposure setting for still images.

This second Live View display option adds the Quick Control screen on the left and a status display at the bottom.

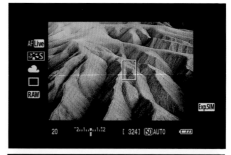

The third display option add a brightness histogram to evaluate exposure.

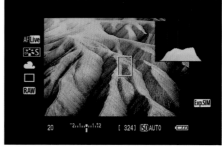

Press DISP. a third time to add a special Quick Control screen on the left side of the LCD. It shows current AF mode Picture Style, white balance, drive mode, image-recording quality/size, AE lock, and a flash ready indicator. In Movie mode the Quick Control screen shows AF mode, Picture Style, Movie-recording size, available or elapsed time and still image-recording quality/size. A final press of DISP. adds a histogram to the screen. The histogram is RGB or brightness, depending on how you have set the histogram option in ▣.

Note: Movie mode has no histogram display.

The Live View Quick Control screen is used similarly to the regular Quick Control screen—press ⊛ and the last adjusted control is highlighted. Use ◄► to choose the setting you want to adjust and then rotate ⌂ to scroll through the options. It is not necessary to use ⊛ to accept the setting; instead, ⊛ is used to exit the Quick Control screen. With the exception of autofocus, all of the settings operate the same as they do in regular shooting.

Autofocus in Live View Shooting

As mentioned previously, when Live View shooting is turned on, the reflex mirror pops up, rendering the viewfinder unusable. Since the autofocus sensors are part of the viewfinder, and the mirror is blocking the viewfinder, the T1i's traditional auto focus method is not immediately functional. Autofocus (AF) is accomplished either by flipping the mirror back down or by evaluating the image coming from the sensor. You choose the AF mode via the Live View function settings screen in ❤️ or via the Live View Quick Control screen.

Note: It is important to understand that when you use Live View shooting, you must explicitly perform the AF function using ✳ (described below), regardless of the AF mode you select. AF is not automatic; it is performed simply by pressing the shutter release button. Each time you engage Live View shooting, the T1i reminds you of autofocus by briefly displaying a message "Perform autofocus with AE lock [✳] button". It is also important to remember to hold down ✳ until the camera beeps to confirm that focus has been achieved.

There are three auto focus options:

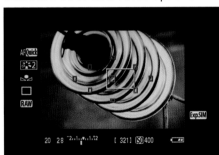

The LCD in Quick AF mode shows the sam e AF points as non-Live View shooting and a magnification rectangle.

Quick Mode AF AFQuick**:** You might wonder why this is called Quick Mode since it takes a bit of time to achieve focus. In reality, the fastest way to achieve focus will most often be Quick Mode. It is also usually the most accurate. The method uses the same autofocus sensors that are used during non-Live View still photography. Remember that during Live

163

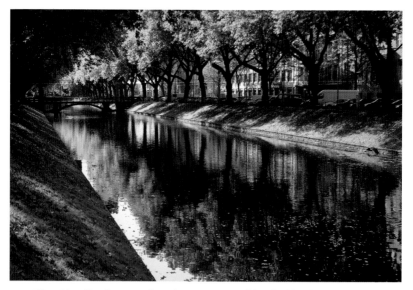

Checking the focus point of your composition in Live View mode is simple; use ⊕ to magnify the image. You can use this method to check focus before you press the shutter button to take the photo.

View, the reflex mirror—reflex is the "R" in SLR—is in the up position so that light lands on the image sensor and creates an image. But because the AF sensors are located in the viewfinder, the reflex mirror must be in the down position so that the light hits the AF sensors. In other words, if you use AF**Quick** the Live View image is temporarily interrupted while the camera sets focus.

When you use AF**Quick**, you must select an AF point, just as you would if you were not using Live View shooting, but you use the Live View Quick Control screen. Press ⊛ to activate the Quick Control screen. Press ▶ AF to highlight the currently selected AF point(s). Use 🔄 to cycle through all of the AF points. If all the points are highlighted, the T1i will select the AF point automatically. There is no shortcut for highlighting all the AF points, just keep scrolling with 🔄. Once you have highlighted the AF point(s) you want to use, press ⊛ or tap the shutter to exit AF point selection. The AF point(s) selected are overlaid on the LCD monitor as gray points.

Note: The AF point selection carries over from non-Live View shooting. For example, if you have selected the center AF point during normal shooting, when you switch to Live View with AF▣▣▣ the selected AF point is the center point until you change it.

Once the AF point is selected, press and hold ✱ to start autofocus. The mirror flips down, interrupting the Live View image on the LCD monitor. The camera then sets focus and confirms the focus with a beep (unless the beep was disabled in ◻▪). Once focus is set, the mirror flips back up and you can see the Live View image again. If you continue to hold down ✱, the AF point used to set focus is highlighted in red.

You can check the focus. A rectangular magnifying frame can be moved anywhere in the scene with ✧. Once in place, press ⊕ to magnify the image in that frame. Press once to magnify 5x, press again to magnify 10x, and press a third time to return to normal view. When focus has been set, press the shutter to take the picture.

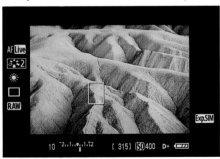

When using Live Mode AF, the AF point is used to select the area of the scene that you want to be in focus. Place it on a section of the image that has high contrast details for best results.

Live Mode AF AF▣▣▣: In this mode, the T1i sets focus by evaluating the image coming from the sensor. The camera uses contrast detection to examine edges in the scene, continually measuring the image while focus is adjusted. This feedback loop takes a bit longer to set focus but it does not interrupt the Live View image.

When you use **AF🔴Live**, first set the Live Mode focus point. When the T1i is in **AF🔴Live**, the white frame overlay becomes the AF point. Use ✧ to move the AF point to the area of the image you want in focus. For quicker and more accurate results, pick an area with high contrast. You can move the AF point around more than 60% of the image with ✧. If you press 🗑—yes, the erase button!—you can reset the AF point to the center of the screen.

Note: You can tell the difference between the magnifying frame in **AF🔴Quick** and the AF point in **AF🔴Live** even though they are both white rectangular boxes. The magnifying frame is larger and has a horizontal aspect ratio. The AF point is smaller and vertical.

Once the AF point is in position, press and hold ✶ to start the AF process. The camera indicates that it has found focus by beeping and turning the AF point green. (If the camera fails to find focus, the AF point turns orange and there is no beep.) You can magnify the image with ⊕ to more critically view the sharpness of the focus. Press ⊕ once to magnify 5x, twice for 10x, and a third time to return to normal view. Once AF is set, the picture can be taken.

Note: If you magnify the image after setting focus, the focus might change.

If there are multiple faces in your scene the AF point will show an arrow on either side to indicate that you can select another face to focus on.

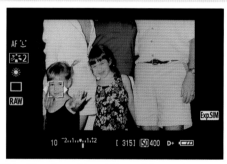

Face Detection AF AF😀: The last Live View AF mode uses face detection technology built into the DIGIC 4 chip. The T1i can detect up to 35 different faces in the scene. Once detected, the camera chooses either the largest or the closest face in the scene and sets the AF point at that location.

When **AF ⚇** is selected, simply frame the scene and the camera detects the faces in it. A special face detection AF point ⌈⌉ appears over the largest or the closest face on the LCD monitor. If there are multiple faces in the scene, the face detection AF point changes to ⟨ ⟩. Use ◄► if you want to move the AF point to a different face. Once a face has been selected, press and hold ✳ to engage the auto focus. When focus is achieved, the face detection AF point turns green and the camera beeps. (If focus cannot be achieved, the AF point turns red.) Once focus has been set the picture can be taken. You cannot magnify the live image to evaluate the focus.

If a face cannot be detected in the scene, the Live Mode AF point appears in the center of the screen and is used for focus. Although you will not be able to reposition this AF point in **AF ⚇**, you can temporarily leave **AF ⚇** by pressing ⌀. The camera switches to **AF🅛🅘🅥🅔** so you can reposition the AF point. Press ⌀ again to return to Face Detection AF mode **AF ⚇**. This is a useful technique to remember if you want to quickly and temporarily switch between Live Mode AF and Face Detection AF.

Face detection is an impressive technology but it is not perfect. Faces that are at an angle to the camera, tilted, too dark or too bright, and those that are too small will be difficult to detect. Don't expect the face detection AF point to completely overlay the face all the time. Also if the lens is way out of focus to begin with, the camera will have difficulty detecting faces. If the lens supports manual focusing (via turning the focus ring), manually set the focus while the lens is in AF mode. Once the Live View image is in better focus, the T1i may detect faces.

Face detection in Live View only occurs near the center area of an image. If the camera detects a face near the edge of the frame, the face detection AF point turns gray. If you attempt autofocus at that time, the center Live View AF point is used instead.

Manual Focus MF: Manual focus is still a good option for Live View shooting. Whether the T1i is in AFQuick, AFLive, or AF ⚲, as soon as you switch the manual focus switch on the lens, the camera displays a magnification frame. One of the best ways to ensure accurate focus is use ✛ to position the frame over the area of your scene that you want in focus. Then press ⊕ to magnify the image either 5x or 10x. Use the focus ring of the lens to set focus, then press ⊕ to restore the normal image size.

Hint: You can center the magnification frame by pressing 🗑.

Focus in Movie Recording

Since movie recording on the T1i uses the same technology as Live View shooting, the AF modes for movie recording are the same as those used for Live View still shooting. You can use Quick Mode AF AFQuick before you start shooting movies, but once recording starts AFQuick is no longer accessible and any press of ✱ attempts focus using AFLive. Live Mode AF AFLive can be used during movie shooting just like with Live View still shooting: use ✛ to move the AF point, then press and hold ✱ to set focus. Face Detection AF AF ⚲ works during movie recording the same way it does for still shooting, too.

Don't expect AFLive or AF ⚲ to be as smooth as if you had a Hollywood-style focus puller (the person whose sole job on a movie set is to adjust lens focus when the camera moves, gently pulling focus from one setting to another). The T1i is designed to achieve focus as quickly as possible. Since there is a feedback loop, the focus setting "hunts" a little when it gets close to the right setting. Also, the brightness level of the scene may temporarily change while focus is being set. If you are used to the autofocus of camcorders it will take some time to adjust to the autofocus of the T1i.

For best results, consider using manual focus when recording movies. It may be the fastest method to achieve focus. With a gentle touch, it can be done while recording.

Note: The built-in microphone may pick up the sound of the focus motors in the lens when the camera adjusts focus.

Exposure

ISO in Live View and Movie Recording

Live View: During Live View still shooting, the ISO speed setting operates the same way as during normal shooting: Press ISO and use 🕸 to select the ISO speed from the display on the LCD monitor.

Note: When Highlight Tone priority has been activated (C.Fn 6), it is indicated by **D+** next to the ISO speed display at the bottom of the LCD monitor during Live View still shooting.

Movie Recording: When you shoot movies you don't have any direct control over the ISO setting. The camera sets it automatically. But the ISO button ISO does have an important function—AE lock. Press ISO and the camera locks the exposure. ✱ appears in the lower left corner of the display. The ISO speed initially starts at ISO 100 and can increase up to 1,600 automatically.

Exposure Modes in Live View and Movie Recording

When you capture stills during Live View shooting, the **P**, **Tv**, **Av**, **M**, and **A-DEP** exposure modes operate the same way as during non-Live View shooting. Exposure compensation is accessed using Av☒ and rotating 🕸 as with normal shooting. But there is no exposure lock. If you want to use auto exposure bracketing (AEB) you'll need to access it through ❏⁚ (see page 152).

Note: Exposure compensation as currently set for non-Live View shooting carries over into Live View shooting.

In 🎥 the T1i automatically sets ISO speed, aperture, and shutter speed. The shutter speed is set in a range from 1/30 to 1/125. The exposure settings will change as needed—even during recording—to maintain a good movie image. Exposure compensation is available and exposure can be locked with ISO. But if you do lock exposure it will stay locked even if the scene gets darker or lighter. In that case you'll need to press ISO to lock a new exposure. If the change is drastic you may need to press ISO twice. You can try to lock down different apertures or shutter speeds using Auto Exposure lock ISO before you start (and during) recording, but there is no option to explicitly set a particular aperture or shutter speed.

Note: If you are going to adjust the zoom while recording, the image may flicker as the T1i adjusts the exposure.

The T1i will display an aperture and shutter speed when the meter is turned on in 📷. This is representative of the settings that will be used if the shutter release button is pressed to take a still picture. It is not necessarily representative of the values that will be used for movie recording.

Metering in Live View and Movie Recording

Metering during Live View shooting is preset to 🔘 because it is linked to the Live View AF point and cannot be changed. You can still use all of the exposure and drive modes, however. Adjust ISO, aperture, shutter speed, and exposure compensation just as you would when shooting normally. When you use a Speedlite external flash unit, E-TTL II metering uses the normal meter in the viewfinder, so the mirror must pop down briefly. When you take a picture with flash, the T1i sounds like it is taking two pictures. Flash units other than Canon do not fire.

Note: If you use Continuous drive mode 🖳, the exposure for all of the images shot is locked to the first image captured.

Movie exposure metering is automatically set for Center-weighted average metering ⊏⊐. The one exception is if you use Face Detection AF **AF** ʚ (see page 166). When a face is

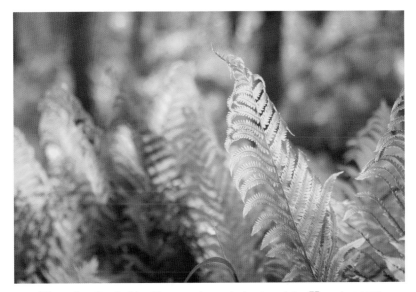

When shooting in Live View mode, metering is set for ⊛ and cannot be changed. Metering in Movie mode is automatically set for ☐, unless you are using AF ⛯ in which case it is set for ⊛.

detected, the metering is Evaluative ⊛ and it is linked to the face detection AF point.

Normally the T1i tries to display a good image on the LCD monitor, no matter how the exposure is set. In Live View, ⟦Exp.SIM⟧ displays to indicate that the image presented on the LCD monitor (in terms of exposure) is close to the actual exposure that will be captured when the shutter release button is pressed. If this icon blinks, it means the image on the screen does not represent the exposure that will be used for the actual image. When shooting movies ⟦Exp.SIM⟧ is replaced by ⟦▶☐⟧ and will also blink if the image displayed on the LCD in not a good representation of the image that will be recorded.

Note: Heat can be a problem when you use the Live View shooting function and movie mode. Thermal build-up on and near the image sensor causes the function to shut down. This is particularly true when you shoot under hot studio lights or outdoors in direct sun. If heat becomes a problem, the temperature icon 🌡 is displayed. While you can keep shooting, image quality may suffer so it is best to turn off Live View shooting for a while.

One T1i feature that is improved with Live View shooting is depth-of-field preview. Normal depth-of-field preview results in a dim viewfinder, making it difficult to see the image. With Live View shooting, as long as the exposure is set for a reasonably correct exposure, when you press the Depth-of-field preview button you see a brighter display that allows you to better check depth of field.

Still Capture during Movie Recording

If you press the shutter release button while recording movies you can capture an image. The image quality/size, white balance and Picture Style will be whatever has been set on the Live View Quick Control screen. The color space will be sRGB (unless shooting RAW), which is the only color space available while shooting movies. The drive mode will be □ and the flash will not fire.

When the image is being captured, the Movie mode will stop to record a high-resolution still frame until the image has been written to the memory card. Typically this takes about a second.

Movie Recording

Recording Movies in 10 Basic Steps

There are ten things you should do to successfully record movies with your T1i. These steps are important because the process of recording movies can be very different than that of shooting stills. These are just a starting point. As you get used to the camera, you'll develop your own steps.

1. Make sure you have plenty of power. If you use batteries, make sure they are charged and make sure you have spares. Running Live View and recording movies can use up battery power quickly. Better yet, use the optional AC adaptor (ACK-E5).

2. Use a large SDHC Class 6 or higher (high-speed) SD memory card. For optimum performance when recording high definition movies, make sure that you format the card in the T1i. If you shoot stills and record movies, consider using different cards for each scenario. This also helps organize files when you download to the computer.

3 Pick the movie resolution: Go to ♈, select [Live View/Movie func. set.] and press ⊛. Highlight [Movie rec. size] and press ⊛. From the drop-down selection, choose 1920x1080 (high definition), 1280x720 (high definition) or 640x480 (standard definition).

4. Enable audio recording: To reduce camera-handling noise picked up by the microphone, make sure that you make all camera adjustments before you start recording.

5. Select a picture style: Press ⊛, highlight the current picture style and use 🖱 to choose from Standard ⬛S, Portrait ⬛P, Landscape ⬛L, Neutral ⬛N, Faithful ⬛F, Monochrome ⬛M, or one of the three User-defined Picture styles ⬛1. Use ◻ to make adjustments—Sharpness, Contrast, Saturation, and Color tone—to the selected Picture Style. (See pages 93-98.)

6. Make a white balance (WB) selection: If in doubt, use ⬛, but the Live View display on the LCD monitor can help you choose the best white balance setting. To set, press ⊛ and highlight the current white balance setting on the LCD monitor. Use 🖱 to scroll through the white balance options: Auto ⬛, Daylight ☀, Shade ⬛, Cloudy ☁, Tungsten light ☀, White Fluorescent light ☰, Flash ϟ, and Custom ◣ (see pages 101-104).

7. Choose a focus mode: Decide if you want to set focus manually or via one of the three special Live View AF modes. If you opt for an AF mode, make sure your lens is not in manual focus mode and then press ⊛, highlight the current AF mode and then use 🖱 to select the AF options: Quick Mode AF **AF Quick**, Live Mode AF **AF Live**, or Face Detection AF **AF ☺**. (See page 163.)

8. Set focus: The T1i does not automatically set focus before movie recording. Press and hold ✱ until you receive a confirmation that focus has been achieved. Depending on the AF mode you have set, this might involve momentary loss of the Live View display on the LCD monitor.

9. Adjust exposure: If you are not happy with the exposure that is set in movie mode, use exposure compensation. Press and hold Av⊠ while rotating 🖱. (See page 150.)

10. Make a test recording: Press ⬜ to start recording. Since you can't monitor audio from the T1i's audio video out terminal while you record movies, make sure that you do a test recording. Listen to the recorded audio to make sure it sounds good and look at the movie to check exposure. Exposure can be adjusted by using ✛ before and during recording.

Movie Recording Parameters

There are four parameters that are important in any digital movie specification: resolution, frame rate, scanning type, and compression.

Resolution: Much like still photography, digital video is captured in pixel form. Unlike stills, however, movies cannot "print" at various sizes and resolutions. Instead, movies are locked into displays that have fixed pixel counts. Rather than talking about how many megapixels a camera has, you specify exactly how many pixels there are in the horizontal and vertical direction.

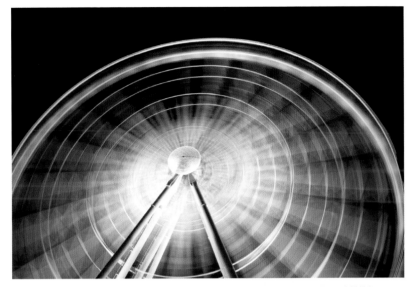

You can make a still image while recording video with the Rebel T1i by simply pressing the shutter button. The movie recording stops briefly—for about one second—to save the image to the memory card.

There are three digital movie resolution options in the T1i: 1920x1080, 1280x720, and 640x480. 1920x1080 and 1280x720 are the two resolutions that comprise high definition video. 640x480 is close to the standard definition digital video specification (which is typically 720x486). It is typical in the "biz" to refer to the resolution by its vertical dimension, so the T1i is considered a 1080 or 720 camera.

The T1i is a true 1080 camera. Some camcorders (including high-level professional cameras costing thousands more) use pixels that are rectangular. The actual count of their pixels is 1440x1080, which is later stretched out to create the 1920-wide image. The T1i uses square pixels.

Frame Rate: The second parameter is frame rate. This should not to be confused with shutter speed or maximum burst rate. It is the number of frames that the camera can capture per second. In the case of the T1i, the camera records 20 frames per second (fps) in 1080 and 30fps in 720 and standard definition. 20fps is a non-standard frame rate for high definition video (which is typically either 30fps or 24fps). So when you shoot at 1080 you may notice that the movie is a little choppy—it stutters a little bit.

Scanning Type: Another parameter important in movies is the scanning type. There is nothing similar to it in still cameras. In the early days of television, bandwidth was a big problem. Transmitting lines of video (think of a line of video as a row of pixels) every 30th of a second required a lot bandwidth. Using lots of bandwidth meant fewer television channels, so a system was devised to transmit every other line of video at 1/60 of a second. This "interlace" scanning scheme has been used for decades and it fit in very nicely with televisions based on CRTs (cathode ray tubes). With the advent of computers and computer displays like LCDs, the concept of interlace scanning became problematic. LCDs are more efficient if they get each line sequentially, rather than every other one. LCDs use a type of scanning that is called progressive. The T1i is a progressive scanning device so the high definition output is sometimes referred to as 1080p or 720p—"p" for "progressive." There are other movie recorders that are 1080i ("i" for "interlace").

Compression: Lastly, because movies—particularly high definition movies—take up a lot of space on memory cards and hard drives, they are usually compressed. Just like the JPEG compression the T1i uses for still images, the video compression is high quality—don't think web movie compression. In video parlance the compression is referred to as a codec, which stands for compressor/decompressor. The T1i uses an MPEG4 compression scheme that is most commonly referred to as h.264. There are a variety of quality levels of h.264, from very low file size and low image quality, to large file size and high image quality. This camera uses a very high quality version of h.264 for all resolutions.

Audio

Audio is recorded simultaneously with the movie. The T1i records one digital audio channel (mono) at a sampling rate of 44.1kHz, which is the same rate used for audio CDs. It uses a linear PCM audio format, which is uncompressed. You can turn off audio recording if it is not needed.

The built-in mic is mono and picks up a lot of the camera noise, like focus motors, stabilization, lens zooming, and any adjustments you make to a camera control. So, if you are going to be handling the camera during movie recording you might consider a separate audio recording device.

Note: There is an automatic audio gain control (AGC) built into the T1i. It is used for controlling the level of the audio recording. It cannot be turned off.

Recording Length

As mentioned before, a large high speed Class 6 SDHC card should be used for movie recording.

Movie rec. size	File size	4GB card	16GB card
1920x1080	330 MB/min.	12 minutes	49 minutes
1280x720	222MB/min	18 minutes	73 minutes
640x480	165 MB/min	24 minutes	99 minutes

The maximum size for a single file is 4GB. If you have installed, say, a 16GB card, when the file size of the current recording reaches 4GB the camera will stop recording. In the chart above, even though the 16GB card has a 49-minute capacity, it would need to be in separate files. On the LCD monitor, the movie recording size information also displays the amount of time left on the memory card. During recording it will indicate the elapsed time of shooting.

If the card you are using is slow, a buffer capacity icon will appear on the LCD monitor. As the buffer fills up, waiting to write to the card, the icon indicates when the buffer is close to reaching capacity. When the memory card is full (or not present) the file recording size on the LCD appears in red.

Movie Playback

To access recorded movies, press ▶. Movies are indicated in the upper right corner of the LCD by 🎬SET and the movie duration in minutes and seconds. Once a movie is selected via 🔄, press ⑤ to enter movie playback mode. A set of "VCR-style" movie controls appears at the bottom of the screen:

Play: This button is highlighted by default. Press ⑤ to begin playback; press it again to pause playback.
Slow motion: Once engaged, use ◀▶ to change the speed of playback

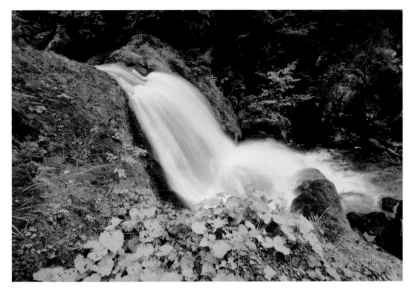

If you know you want to record movie files, make sure to pack several large SDHC memory cards in your camera bag.

First frame: Returns to first frame of the recorded movie.
Previous frame: Highlight this button and press ⊛ to move back one frame. If you keep holding down ⊛, the movie will speed up until you reach "rewind" speed.
Next frame: Operates exactly like "Previous frame" except it advances through frames rather than going backwards.
Last frame: Moves to the last frame of the movie.

While movies are playing back, rotate ⌂ to adjust the volume of the audio coming out of the camera's speaker. The control will not affect the volume when the T1i is connected to a TV (see page 89). In that case, use the volume control on the TV.

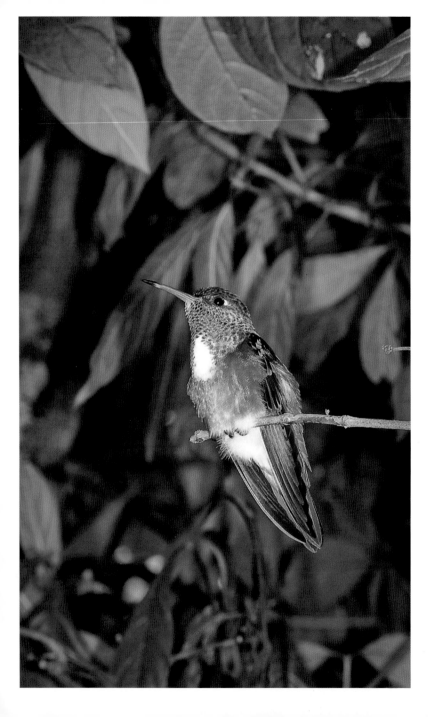

Flash

Electronic flash is not just a supplement for low light; it can also be a wonderful tool for creative photography. Flash is highly controllable, its color is precise, and the results are repeatable. However, the challenge is getting the right look. Many photographers shy away from using flash because they aren't happy with the results. This is because on-camera flash can be harsh and unflattering, and taking the flash off the camera used to be a complicated procedure with less than sure results.

The Canon EOS Rebel T1i's sophisticated flash system eliminates many of these concerns and, of course, the LCD monitor gives instantaneous feedback, alleviating the guesswork. With digital, you take a picture and you know immediately whether or not the lighting is right. You can then adjust the light level higher or lower, change the angle, soften the light, color it, and more. Just think of the possibilities:

Fill Flash—Fill in harsh shadows in all sorts of conditions and use the LCD monitor to see exactly how well the fill flash works. Often, you'll want to dial down the output of an accessory flash to make sure the fill is natural looking.

Off-Camera Flash—Putting a flash on a dedicated flash cord allows you to move the flash away from the camera and still have it work automatically. Using the LCD monitor, you can see exactly what the effects are so you can move the flash up or down, left or right, for the best light and shadows on your subject.

Using an accessory flash might seem intimidating to photographers new to using a D-SLR, but it is a limitless tool that allows you to add and manipulate the light source to best capture your photographic subject.

Close-Up Flash—This used to be a real problem, except for those willing to spend some time experimenting. Now you can see exactly what the flash does to the subject. This works fantastically well with off-camera flash, as you can "feather" the light (aim it so it doesn't hit the subject directly) to gain control over its strength and how it lights the area around the subject.

Multiple Flashes—Modern flash systems have made exposure with multiple flashes easier and more accurate. However, since the flash units are not on continuously, they can be hard to place so that they light the subject properly. Not anymore. With the Rebel T1i, it is easy to set up the flash, and then take a test shot. Does it look good, or not? Make changes if you need to. In addition, this camera lets you use certain EX-series flash units (and independent brands with the same capabilities) that offer wireless exposure control. This is a good way to learn how to master multiple-flash setups.

Colored Light—Many flashes look better with a slight warming filter, but that is not what this tip is about. With multiple light sources, you can attach colored filters (also called gels) to the various flashes so that different colors light different parts of the photo. (This can be a very trendy look.)

Balancing Mixed Lighting—Architectural and corporate photographers have long used added light to fill in dark areas of a scene so it looks less harsh. Now you can double-check the light balance on your subject using the LCD monitor. You can even be sure the added light is the right color by attaching filters to the flash to mimic or match lights (such as a green filter to match fluorescents).

Flash Synchronization

The Rebel T1i is equipped with an electromagnetically timed, vertically traveling focal-plane shutter that forms a slit to expose the sensor as it moves across it. With a focal-plane shutter, the entire surface of the sensor is not exposed at one time when shutter speeds shorter than the flash duration (sync) are used. So, if you use flash with a shutter speed that is shorter than the maximum flash sync speed, the flash illuminates the scene for a shorter time than the sensor is exposed, and you get a partially exposed picture. However, at shutter speeds below the maximum sync speed, the whole sensor surface is exposed at some point to accept the flash.

The Rebel T1i's maximum flash sync speed is 1/200 second. If you use a flash and set the exposure to a speed faster than that in **Tv** or **M** mode, the camera automatically resets the speed to 1/200. In **Av** the T1i won't let you go faster than 1/200. Instead, the shutter speed flashes 1/200 if the aperture setting will cause overexposure.

The camera also offers high-speed sync with EX-series flash units that allow flash at all shutter speeds (even 1/4000 second where, basically, the flash fires continuously as the slit goes down the sensor). High-speed synchronization must be activated on the flash unit itself or by using the Flash control menu and is indicated by a ⚡H symbol on the flash unit's LCD panel and in the T1i's viewfinder. See the flash manual for specific information on using high-speed flash sync.

Guide Numbers

It is helpful to compare guide numbers (GN) when you shop for a flash unit because the GN is a simple way to state the power of the unit. It is computed as the product of aperture value and subject distance and is usually included in the manufacturer's specifications for the unit. High numbers indicate more power; however, this is not a linear relationship. Guide numbers act a little like f/stops (because they are directly related to f/stops!); e.g., 56 is half the power of 80, or 110 is twice the power of 80 (see the relationship with f/5.6, f/8, and f/11?).

Since guide numbers are expressed in meters and/or feet, distance is part of the guide number formula. Also, guide numbers are usually based on ISO 100 (film or sensor sensitivity), but this can vary, so check the ISO speed reference (and determine whether the GN was calculated using feet or meters) when you compare different flash units. If you compare units that have zoom-head diffusers (special lenses built into the flash units to match flash angle with lens angle of view), make sure you compare the guide numbers for similar zoom-head settings.

Built-in Flash

The Rebel T1i's built-in flash pops open to a higher position than the flash on many other cameras. This reduces the chance of getting red-eye and minimizes problems with large lenses blocking the flash. The flash supports E-TTL II (an evaluative autoexposure system), covers a field of view up to a 17mm focal length and has a guide number of 43/13 (ISO 100, in feet/meters). Like most built-in flashes, it is not particularly high-powered, but its advantage is that it is always available and is useful as fill-flash to modify ambient light. Key to this flash and to many Canon Speedlites, is the flash's ability to send color data to the camera's processor each time it fires. This helps the system measure many variables so it can better maintain consistent color.

The flash pops up automatically in low-light or backlit situations in the following Basic Zone exposure modes: ▢, ⚘, ⚘, and ⛰. It does not activate in ▲, ⚞, or ⚟ modes. In the Creative Zone and ⚙ of the Basic Zone, you can choose to use the flash (or not) at any time. Just press the ⚡ button (located on the front of the camera, on the upper left of the lens mount housing) and the flash pops up. To turn it off, simply push the flash down.

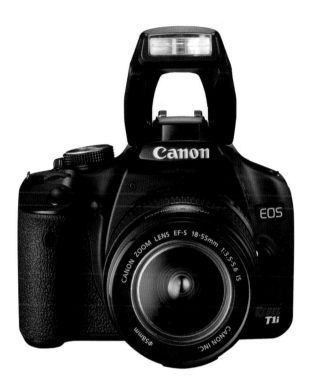

The Rebel T1i comes equipped with a built-in flash. The built-in flash is a perfect tool for filling in dark shadows (also called fill flash) and freezing movement when shooting with slower shutter speeds.

The Creative Zone exposure modes do not all use the same approach with the built-in flash. In **P** mode, the flash is fully automatic, setting both an appropriate shutter speed and the aperture. In **Tv**, it can be used when you need a specific shutter speed. In **Av**, if you set an aperture that the flash uses for its exposure, the shutter speed influences how much of the ambient (or natural) light appears in the image. In **M**, you set the aperture to control flash exposure, then choose a shutter speed that is appropriate for the ambient light in the scene (see flash metering below). Remember, you can use any shutter speed of 1/200 second and slower unless using high-speed sync.

Flash Metering

The Rebel T1i uses an evaluative autoexposure system that measures light coming through the lens or TTL. Canon's first evaluative flash metering system was called E-TTL, The latest version is called E-TTL II (first introduced with the pro-level Canon EOS-1D Mark II camera). The system has improved algorithms and, compared to earlier models, can better use distance information obtained from the lens to improve control over flash exposure. It is important to understand that E-TTL II is a system—it won't work unless you are using both a Canon Speedlite that supports E-TTL II and a Canon EOS camera that supports E-TTL II.

To understand the Rebel T1i's flash metering, you need to understand how a flash works with a digital camera on automatic. The camera causes the flash to fire twice for the exposure. First, a preflash is fired to analyze exposure. Then the flash fires during the actual exposure, creating the image. During the preflash, the camera's Evaluative metering system measures the light reflected back from the subject. Once it senses that the light is sufficient, it cuts off the flash and takes the actual exposure with the same flash duration. The amount of flash that hits the subject is based on how long the flash is on; close subjects receive shorter flash bursts than more distant subjects. This double flash system works quite well, but you may also find that it causes some subjects to react by closing their eyes during the real exposure. However, they will be well exposed!

Flash can be confusing when you are trying to set exposure but there are key concepts that, once understood, will help you determine how to adjust exposure when using flash. First off, shutter speed has no effect on flash exposure (unless you go above the sync speed—1/200—where the image will be unusable). The flash only occurs for a brief moment—so keeping the shutter open longer won't let in any more light coming from the flash because it has already finished lighting up the scene. A slower shutter speed merely lets in more ambient light.

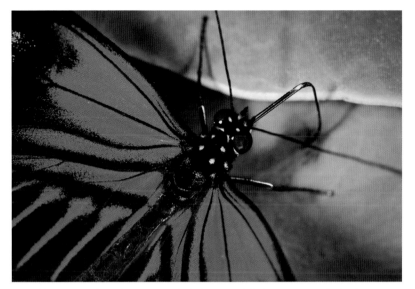

Using flash for close-up work helps to minimize camera shake from hand-holding, as well as properly exposing subjects.

Second, aside from controlling the flash power output on the flash unit itself, the only way to control the amount of flash illumination is to change the aperture. If you open up the aperture, you let more flash light onto the sensor. You will also allow more ambient light, but most times the ambient light is at a much lower level so the change may not be as noticeable.

So remember: adjust the shutter speed to control the amount of ambient light and adjust the aperture to control the amount of flash illumination. Try it out yourself. Photograph a scene with some ambient light. Use **M** exposure mode and adjust only the shutter speed (in both directions). What changes do you see in your image? Now repeat the exercise but adjust only the aperture.

Flash with Camera Exposure Modes

With the exception of Creative Auto ⊡ you have no control over flash when the camera is set in the Basic Zone. This means you have no say in whether the flash is used for an exposure or how the exposure is controlled. The camera determines it all depending on how it senses the scene's light values. When the light is dim or there is a strong back-light, the built-in flash automatically pops up and fires, except in ⛰, ❀, and ⛻ modes. With ⊡ your choices are letting the camera determine when to use flash (Auto) ⚡ᴬ, use flash always ⚡, or never use flash ⊕.

In the Creative Zone, you either pop up the built-in flash by pushing the ⚡ button on the front left of the camera, or you attach an EX Speedlite accessory flash unit and simply switch it to the "ON" position. The flash operates in the various Creative Zone modes as detailed below.

Program AE P

Flash photography can be used for any photo where supple-mentary light is needed. All you have to do is turn on the flash unit—the camera does the rest automatically. Canon Speedlite EX flash units should be switched to E-TTL II and the ready light should be on, indicating that the flash is ready to fire. While shooting, you must pay attention to make sure the flash symbol ⚡ is visible in the viewfinder, indicating that the flash is charged when you are ready to take your picture. The Rebel T1i picks a shutter speed in the range of 1/60–1/200 second automatically in **P** mode and also selects the correct aperture.

Shutter-Priority AE Tv

This mode is a good choice in situations when you are using flash and want to control the shutter speed. In **Tv** mode, you set the shutter speed before or after a dedicated accessory flash is turned on. All shutter speeds between 1/200 second and 30 seconds synchronize with the flash. With E-TTL II flash in **Tv** mode, synchronization with longer shutter speeds is a creative choice that allows you to control the ambient-light background exposure. A portrait of a person at dusk that is shot with conventional TTL flash in front of a building with its lights on would illuminate the person correctly but would cause the background to go dark. However, using **Tv** mode, you can control the exposure of the background by changing the shutter speed. (A tripod is recommended to keep the camera stable during long exposures).

If the aperture value flashes on the LCD or in the viewfinder, the current shutter speed is forcing an aperture value beyond what the lens can produce. Adjust the shutter speed until the aperture value stops blinking.

Aperture-Priority AE Av

Using this mode you can balance the flash with existing light, controlling depth of field in the composition. By selecting the aperture, you are also able to influence the range of the flash. The aperture is selected by turning ✺ and watching the external flash's LCD panel until the desired range appears. The camera calculates the lighting conditions and automatically sets the correct shutter speed for the ambient light. If the shutter speed value flashes on the LCD or in the viewfinder, the camera wants to choose a shutter speed beyond the sync speed of the flash. Either set the flash for high-speed sync or close down the aperture.

Manual Exposure M

Going Manual gives you the greatest number of choices in modifying exposure. The photographer who prefers to adjust everything manually can determine the relationship of ambient light and electronic flash by setting both the aperture and shutter speed. Any aperture on the lens and all shutter speeds between 1/200 second and 30 seconds can be used. If a shutter speed above the normal flash sync speed is set, unless the flash is set to high-speed sync the Rebel T1i switches automatically to 1/200 second to prevent partial exposure of the sensor.

M mode also offers a number of creative possibilities for using flash in connection with long shutter speeds. You can use zooming effects with a smeared background and a sharply rendered main subject, or take photographs of objects in motion with a sharp "flash core" and indistinct outlines.

A-DEP A-DEP

Using flash with **A-DEP** is the same as shooting in **P** mode.

FE (Flash Exposure) Lock

Autoexposure lock (AE lock, see page 149) on the T1i is a useful tool for controlling exposure in difficult natural light situations. Flash exposure (FE) lock offers the same control in difficult flash situations. When either the pop-up flash or an attached flash is turned on, you can lock the flash exposure by pressing the FE lock button ✳. (This is the same as the AE lock button located on the back of the camera toward the upper right corner.)

With a charged external or pop-up flash active, pressing FE lock causes the camera to emit a preflash, and the T1i calculates the exposure without taking the shot. **FEL** appears briefly in the viewfinder (replacing the shutter speed) during the pre-flash. The ⚡ changes to ⚡*, indicating the flash exposure has been locked. You can press ✳ repeatedly as you change framing. If the subject is beyond the illumination of the flash, ⚡ blinks.

Note: FE lock can also be used to reduce people's reactions to the preflash. They may keep their eyes open during the actual exposure for a change!

To use the FE lock, pop up the flash (or turn on an external flash unit), and then lock focus on your subject by pressing the shutter button halfway. Next, aim the center of the viewfinder at the important part of the subject and press the FE lock button. (⚡* appears in the viewfinder.) Now, reframe your composition and take the picture. FE lock produces quite accurate flash exposures.

Using the same principle, you can make the flash weaker or stronger. Instead of pointing the viewfinder at the subject to set flash exposure, point it at something light in tone or a subject closer to the camera. This causes the flash to provide less exposure. For more light, aim the camera at something black or far away. With a little experimenting, and by reviewing the LCD monitor, you can very quickly establish appropriate flash control for particular situations.

Flash Exposure Compensation
You can also use the Rebel T1i's flash exposure compensation feature to adjust flash exposure by up to +/- 2 stops in 1/3-stop increments (or 1/2-stop increments if selected in C.Fn 1; see page 74). Flash exposure compensation operates similarly to the regular exposure compensation and is accessed via ❏⁺: First highlight [Flash control] and press ⑧. Next, highlight [Built-in flash func. setting] for the pop-up flash or [External flash func. setting] for an external flash and press ⑧ again. Finally, select [Flash exp. comp] and press ⑧ yet again. A flash exposure compensation scale is displayed that operates similarly to the exposure compensation scale (page 150). The viewfinder displays 🔲 to let you know flash exposure compensation is enabled. The shooting settings display also shows 🔲 and the amount of compensation.

Note: If you have learned to use the Quick Control Screen you can quickly set flash exposure compensation. With the shooting settings displayed on the LCD, press ⑧. Use ✧ to highlight the flash exposure compensation display. Then use 🎛 to adjust the setting. If you want to have a little guidance for the setting, after it is highlighted, press ⑧ to bring up a more intuitive adjustment screen.

For the most control over flash, use the camera's **M** exposure setting. Set an exposure that is correct overall for the scene, and then turn on the flash. (The flash exposure is still E-TTL II automatic.) The shutter speed (as long as it is 1/200 second or slower) controls the overall light from the scene (and the total exposure). The f/stop controls the exposure of the flash. So, to a degree, you can make the overall scene

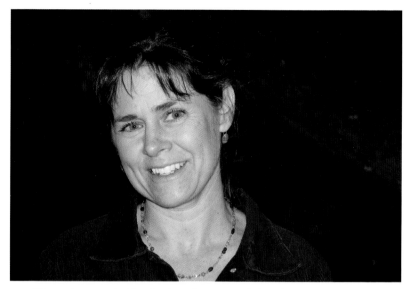

The red-eye reduction tool works very well for shots taken with the Rebel T1i's built-in flash unit. © Kevin Kopp

lighter or darker by changing shutter speed (up to 1/200 second), with no direct effect on the flash exposure. (Note, however, that this does not work with high-speed flash.)

Red-Eye Reduction

In low-light conditions when the flash is close to the axis of the lens (which is typical for built-in flashes), the flash reflects back from the retina of people's eyes (because their pupils are wide). This appears as "red-eye" in the photo. You can reduce the chances of red-eye appearing by using an off-camera flash or by having the person look at a bright light before you shoot (to cause their pupils to constrict). In addition, many cameras offer a red-eye reduction feature that causes the flash to fire a burst of light before the actual exposure, resulting in contraction of the subject's pupils. Unfortunately, this may also result in less than flattering expressions from your subject.

Although the Rebel T1i's flash pops up higher than most, red eye may still be a problem. The Rebel T1i also offers a red-eye reduction feature for flash exposures, but the feature works differently than red-eye reduction on many other cameras. The Rebel T1i uses a continuous light from a bulb next to the handgrip, just below the shutter button—be careful not to block it with your fingers.

A continuous lower power light versus a brief bright flash helps your subject pose with better expressions. Red-eye reduction is set in the ◘˙ menu under [Red-eye On/Off]. Since the lamp is lower power, it takes a little longer to do the job. The T1i provides a visual countdown in the viewfinder, where the exposure compensation scale would normally display. Once the indicator decrements to nothing and the exposure compensation scale reappears, you can take the picture. In reality, you can take the picture at any time, but for best results wait for the countdown.

Note: Don't confuse red-eye reduction with the AF-assist beam (see page 120). The AF-assist beam uses a series of brief flashes to help the T1i achieve focus. This function is turned on/off via C.Fn 8, AF assist beam firing, not the red-eye reduction setting.

Canon Speedlite EX Flash Units

Canon offers a range of accessory flash units in the EOS system, called Speedlites. While Canon Speedlites don't replace studio strobes, they are remarkably versatile. These highly portable flash units can be mounted in the camera's hot shoe or used off camera with a dedicated cord.

The Rebel T1i is compatible with the EX-series of Speedlites. Units in the EX-series range in power from the Speedlite 580EX II, which has a maximum GN of 190/58 (ISO 100, in feet/meters), to the small and compact Speedlite 220EX, which has a GN of 72/22 (ISO 100, in feet/meters).

Speedlite EX-series flash units offer a wide range of features to expand your creativity. They are designed to work with the camera's microprocessor to take advantage of E-TTL II exposure control, extending the abilities of the Rebel T1i considerably.

I strongly recommend Canon's off-camera extension cord for your flash, the shoe cord OC-E3. When you use this, the flash can be moved away from the camera for more interesting light and shadow. You can aim light toward the side or top of a close-up subject for variations in contrast and color. If you find that your subject is overexposed, rather than dialing down the flash (which can be done on certain flash units), just aim the flash a little farther away from the subject so it doesn't get hit so directly by the light.

Canon Speedlite 580EX II
Introduced with the EOS 1D Mark III professional camera, the 580EX II replaces the popular 580EX. This top-of-the-line flash unit offers outstanding range and features adapted to digital cameras. Improvements over the 580EX include a stronger quick-locking hot shoe connection, stronger battery door, dust and water resistance, a shorter and quieter recycling time, and an external metering sensor. The tilt/swivel zoom head on the 580EX II covers focal lengths from 14mm to 105mm, and it swivels a full 180° in either direction. The zoom positions (which correspond to the focal lengths 24, 28, 35, 50, 70, 80, and 105mm) can be set manually or automatically (the flash reflector zooms with the lens). In addition, this flash "knows" what size sensor is used with a D-SLR and it varies its zoom accordingly. With the built-in retractable diffuser in place, the flash coverage is wide enough for a 14mm lens. It provides a high flash output with a GN of 190/58 (at ISO 100 in feet/meters) when the zoom head is positioned at 105mm. The guide number decreases as the angular coverage increases for shorter focal lengths, but is still quite high with a GN of 145/44 (ISO 100 in feet/meters) at 50mm, or a GN of 103/32 (ISO 100 in feet/meters) at 28mm. When used with other flashes, the 580EX II can function as either a master flash or a slave unit (see page 199).

Also new to the 580EX II is a PC terminal for use with PC cords. PC cords were the way external flashes were connected to cameras before the hotshoe was developed. The T1i does not have a PC connector. But PC terminals are still used for flash accessories like wireless remotes. For external power, a new power pack, LP-E4, has been developed for the 580EX II that is dust and water-resistant.

The large, illuminated LCD panel on the 580EX II provides clear information on all settings: flash function, reflector position, working aperture, and flash range in feet or meters. The flash also includes a Select dial for easier selection of these settings. When you press the T1i's Depth-of-field preview button (front of camera, on lower right of the lens mount housing), a one-second burst of light is emitted. This modeling flash allows you to judge the effect of the flash. The 580EX II also has 14 user-defined custom settings that are totally independent of the camera's Custom Functions; for more information, see the flash manual.

While the LCD panel on the 580EX II provides a lot of information, it can be a little complicated if you try to adjust the various settings and custom functions when you don't use the flash every day. Canon came up with a great solution: You can use the T1i menu system to access the 580EX II's controls. The Custom Functions appear as numeric codes on the Speedlite's LCD. Within the T1i External flash control system, however, those Custom Functions have names and descriptions, just like the T1i's own Custom Functions. The same is true when you adjust other flash functions such as Flash mode, Flash Exposure Compensation, Flash Exposure Bracketing and many more. You can also adjust the flash zoom head setting and wireless E-TTL II setting from the camera. With this new intelligence, it has never been easier to learn how to use Canon Speedlites to capture great images.

Canon Speedlite 430EX II
Much as the 580EX II improved on the 580EX, the 430EX II, introduced in June of 2008, improves on the 430EX. While the GN stays the same—141/43 (ISO 100 in feet/meters) the

recycle time has increased by 20%. It is also quieter than the 430EX and can be controlled from the T1i, just like the 580EX II. It offers E-TTL II flash control, wireless E-TTL operation, flash exposure compensation, and high-speed synchronization. It does not offer flash exposure bracketing.

The tilt/swivel zoom reflector covers focal lengths from 24 to 105mm and swivels 180 degrees in each direction. The zoom head operates automatically for focal lengths of 24, 28, 35, 50, 70, 80, and 105mm. A built-in wide-angle pull-down reflector makes flash coverage wide enough for a 14mm lens.

An LCD panel on the rear of the unit makes adjusting settings easy, and there are six Custom Functions. Just like the 580EX II, you can control most of the settings and custom functions from the T1i menus. Since the 430EX II supports wireless E-TTL, it can be used as a remote (slave) unit. A new quick-release mounting system makes it easy to securely attach the 430EX II to the T1i.

Canon Speedlite 430EX

The 430EX is less complicated, more compact, and less expensive than the top models. It offers E-TTL II flash control, wireless E-TTL operation (slave only), flash exposure compensation, and high-speed synchronization. The 430EX flash unit provides high performance with an ISO 100 GN of 141 in feet (43 in meters) with the zoom reflector set for 105mm (somewhat weaker than the 580EX II, but still quite powerful).

The tilt/swivel zoom reflector covers focal lengths from 24 to 105mm. The zoom head operates automatically for focal lengths of 24, 28, 35, 50, 70, 80, and 105mm. A built-in, wide-angle pull-down reflector makes flash coverage wide enough for a 17mm lens.

An LCD panel on the rear of the unit makes adjusting settings easy, and there are six Custom Functions. However, the 430EX does not offer the menu control from the T1i that the 580EX II and 430EX II do. If you are new to using Canon

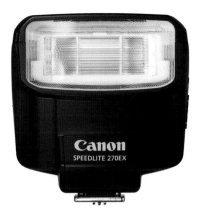

Canon Speedlite 270EX

Speedlites and aren't good about remembering custom function codes, I recommend spending a little more money for the 430EX II. If not, the 430EX does support wireless E-TTL and it can be used as a slave unit.

Canon Speedlite 270EX

If you are looking for a simple, small flash that fits into just about every camera bag or even your pocket, the 270EX is it. The 270EX was introduced at the same time that the T1i was. It is a compact basic flash unit that still offers a lot of features despite its size. Rather than have a zoom reflector, it has a 2-step selection of 28mm and 50mm. At the 28mm setting it has a guide number of 72 in feet, 22 in meters at ISO 100. At the 50mm position the GN is 89 feet, 27 meters at ISO 100.

Unlike it predecessor (220EX), the 270EX has a bounce feature where the flash head can rotate to point straight up. It can also be controlled from the T1i menu system.

Other Speedlites

The Speedlite 220EX is an economy alternative EX-series flash. It offers E-TTL flash and high-speed sync, but does not offer E-TTL II, wireless E-TTL flash, bounce and it can't be controlled by the camera menu.

Close-Up Flash

There are also two specialized flash units for close-up photography that work well with the EOS Rebel T1i. Both provide direct light on the subject.

Macro Twin Lite MT-24EX: The MT-24EX uses two small
flashes affixed to a ring that attaches to the lens. These can
be adjusted to different positions to alter the light and can
be used at different strengths so one can be used as a main
light and the other as a fill light. If both flash tubes are
switched on, they produce a GN of 72/22 (ISO 100 in
feet/meters), and when used individually, the guide number
is 36/11 (feet/meters). It does an exceptional job with direc-
tional lighting in macro shooting.

Macro Ring Lite MR-14EX: Like the MT-24EX, the MR-14EX
uses two small flashes affixed to a ring. It has a GN of 46/14
(ISO 100 in feet/meters), and both flash tubes can be inde-
pendently adjusted in 13 steps from 1:8 to 8:1. It is a flash
that encircles the lens and provides illumination on axis with
it. This results in nearly shadowless photos because the
shadow falls behind the subject compared to the lens position, though there will be shadow effects along curved edges.
It is often used to show fine detail and color in a subject, but
it cannot be used for varied light and shadow effects. This
flash is commonly used in medical and dental photography so
that important details are not obscured by shadows.

The power pack for both of these specialized flash units
fits into the flash shoe of the camera. In addition, both
macro flash units offer some of the same technical features
as the 580EX II, including E-TTL operation, wireless E-TTL
flash, and high-speed synchronization.

Note: When the Rebel T1i is used with older system flash
units (such as the EZ series), the flash unit must be set to
manual, and TTL does not function. For this reason, Canon
EX Speedlite system flash units are recommended for use
with the camera.

Bounce Flash

Direct flash can often be harsh and unflattering, causing heavy shadows behind the subject or underneath features such as eyebrows and bangs. Bouncing the flash softens the light and creates a more natural-looking light effect. The Canon Speedlite 580EX II, 580EX, 430EX II, 430EX and 270EX accessory flash units feature heads that are designed to tilt so that a shoe-mounted flash can be aimed at the ceiling to produce soft, even lighting. The 580EX II also swivels 180° in both directions, while the 430EX II swivels 180° to the left and 90° to the right. This allows the light to be bounced off something to the side of the camera, like a wall or reflector. However, the ceiling or wall must be white or neutral gray, or it may cause an undesirable color cast in the finished photo.

Wireless E-TTL Flash

With the Wireless E-TTL feature, you can use up to three groups of Speedlite 580EX IIs, 430EX IIs, 430EXs, or the now discontinued 580EXs, 550EXs, and 420EXs, for more natural lighting or emphasis. (The number of flash groups is limited to three, but the number of actual flash units is unlimited.) The master unit and the camera control the exposure. When you use the 580EX II, you can set it to be the master, controlling all the other flashes, or a slave. The 430EX II and 430EX can only be used as a remote (slave) unit. Other wireless flash options include the Speedlite infrared transmitter (ST-E2), which only acts as a controller mounted on the T1i (it does not emit light to illuminate a scene), or the Macro Twin Lite MT-24EX and the Macro Ring Lite MR-14EX.

For wireless E-TTL, a 580EX II, MT-24EX, MR-14EX or either 580EX or 550EX (both discontinued) is mounted in the flash shoe and set to function as a master unit. Slave units are set up in the surrounding area. The light ratio of slave units can be varied manually or automatically. With E-TTL (wireless) control, several Speedlite can be controlled at once.

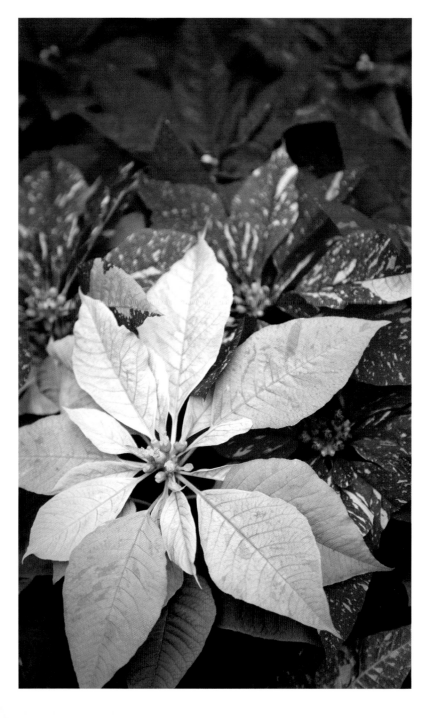

Lenses and Accessories

The Rebel T1i belongs to an extensive family of Canon EOS-compatible equipment, including lenses, flashes, and other accessories. With this wide range of available options, you can expand the capabilities of your camera quite easily. Canon has long had an excellent reputation for its lenses, and offers over 60 different lenses to choose from. Several independent manufacturers offer quality Canon-compatible lenses as well.

The Rebel T1i can use both Canon EF and EF-S lenses, ranging from wide-angle to tele-zoom, as well as single-focal-length lenses—from very wide to extreme telephoto. Keep in mind, however, that standard 35mm focal lengths act differently on many D-SLRs than they did with film. This is because many digital sensors are smaller than a frame of 35mm film, so they crop the area seen by the lens, essentially creating a different format. Effectively, this magnifies the subject within the image area of the Rebel T1i and results in the lens acting as if it has been multiplied by a factor of 1.6 compared to 35mm film cameras.

So, both the widest angle and the farthest zoom focal lengths are multiplied by the Rebel T1i's 1.6x focal length conversion factor. The EF 14mm f/2.8 L lens, for example, is a super-wide lens when used with a 35mm film camera or a full-framed sensor like that found in the EOS 5D Mark II, but offers the 35mm-format equivalent of a 22mm wide-angle lens (14 multiplied by 1.6) when attached to the EOS Rebel T1i—wide, but not super-wide. On the other hand, put a 400mm lens on the Rebel T1i and you get the equivalent of a 640mm telephoto—a big boost with no change in aperture. (Be sure to use a tripod for these focal lengths!)

High-quality lenses can make a huge impact on your photography in terms of quality as well as precision.

It is interesting to note that this is exactly the same thing that happens when one focal length is used with different sized film formats. For example, a 50mm lens is considered a mid-range focal length for 35mm, but it would be a wide-angle lens for medium format cameras. The focal length of the lens doesn't really change, but the field of view that the camera captures changes. In other words, this isn't an artifact of digital photography, it's just physics!

Note: Unless stated otherwise, I refer to the actual focal length of a lens throughout the rest of the chapter, not its 35mm equivalent.

Choosing Lenses

The focal length and design of a lens have a huge effect on how you photograph. The correct lens makes photography a joy; the wrong one makes you leave the camera at home. One approach for choosing a lens is to determine if you are frustrated with your current lens. Do you constantly want to see more of the scene than the lens allows? Then consider a wider-angle lens. Is the subject too small in your photos? Then look into acquiring a zoom or telephoto lens. Do you need more light-gathering ability? Maybe a fixed-focal length lens is needed.

Certain subjects lend themselves to specific focal lengths. Wildlife and sports action are best photographed using focal lengths of 200mm or more, although nearby action can be managed with focal lengths as short as 125mm. Portraits look great when shot with focal lengths between 50 and 65mm. Interiors often demand wide-angle lenses, such as 12mm. Many people also like wide-angles for landscapes, but telephotos can come in handy for distant scenes. Close-ups can be shot with nearly any focal length, though skittish subjects such as butterflies might need a rather long lens.

The inherent magnification factor is great news for the photographer who needs long focal lengths for wildlife or

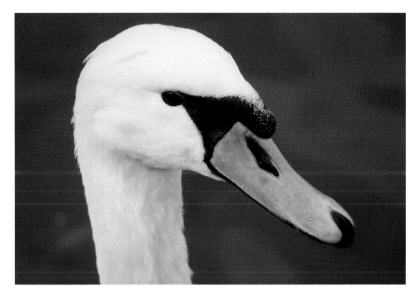

Telephoto lenses help isolate your subject in the frame by removing potentially distracting background elements.

sports. A standard 300mm lens for 35mm film now acts like a 480mm lens on the Rebel T1i. You get a long focal length in a smaller lens, often with a wider maximum f/stop, and with a much lower price tag. But this news is tough for people who need wide-angles, since the width of what the digital camera sees is significantly cropped in comparison to what a 35mm camera would see using the same lens. You need lenses with shorter focal lengths to see the same amount of wide-angle you may have been used to with film.

Zoom vs. Prime Lenses

When zoom lenses first came on the market, they were not even close to a single-focal-length lens in sharpness, color rendition, or contrast. Today, you can get superb image quality from either type. There are some important differences, though. The biggest is maximum f/stop.

Zoom lenses are rarely as fast (meaning that they rarely have as big a maximum aperture) as single-focal-length (prime) lenses. A 28-200mm zoom lens, for example, might have a maximum aperture at 200mm of f/5.6, yet a single-focal-length lens might be f/4 or even f/2.8. When zoom lenses come close to a single-focal-length lens in f/stops, they are usually considerably bigger and more expensive than the single-focal-length lens. Of course, they also offer a whole range of focal lengths, which a single-focal-length lens cannot do. There is no question that zoom lenses are versatile.

EF-Series Lenses

Canon EF lenses include some unique technologies. Canon pioneered the use of tiny autofocus motors in its lenses. In order to focus swiftly, the focusing elements within the lens need to move with quick precision. Canon developed the lens-based ultrasonic motor for this purpose. This technology makes the lens motor spin with ultrasonic oscillation energy instead of the conventional drive-train system (which tends to be noisy). This allows lenses to autofocus nearly instantly with no noise, and it uses less battery power than traditional systems. Canon lenses that use this motor are labeled USM. (Lower-priced Canon lenses have small motors in the lenses too, but they don't use USM technology, and can be slower and noisier.)

Canon is also a pioneer in the use of image-stabilizing technologies. IS (Image Stabilizer) lenses utilize sophisticated motors and sensors to adapt to slight movement during exposure. It's pretty amazing—the lens actually has vibration-detecting gyrostabilizers that move a special image-stabilizing lens group in response to lens movement. This dampens movement that occurs from handholding a camera and allows much slower shutter speeds to be used. IS also allows big telephoto lenses (such as the EF 500mm IS lens) to be used on tripods that are lighter than would normally be used with non-IS telephoto lenses.

The IS technology is part of many zoom lenses, and does a great job overall. However, IS lenses in the mid-focal length ranges have tended to be slower zooms matched against single-focal-length lenses. For example, compare the EF 28-135mm f/3.5-5.6 IS lens to the EF 85mm f/1.8. The former has a great zoom range, but allows less light at maximum aperture. At 85mm (a good focal length for people), the EF 28-135mm is an f/4 lens, more than two stops slower than the f/1.8 single-focal-length lens, when both are shot "wide-open" (typical of low-light situations). While you could make up the two stops in "handholdability" due to the IS technology, that also means you must shoot two full shutter speeds slower, which can be a real problem in stopping subject movement.

EF-S Series Lenses

EF lenses are the standard lenses for all Canon EOS cameras. EF-S lenses are small, compact lenses designed for use on digital SLRs with smaller-type sensors (such as the EOS 20D, 30D, 40D, 50D, the EOS Digital Rebel, the Rebel XT, the Rebel XTi, the Rebel XS, the Rebel XSi and now the Rebel T1i). They were introduced with the EF-S 18-55mm lens packaged with the original EOS Digital Rebel. They cannot be used with film EOS cameras or with any of the EOS-1D cameras (1D Mark III, 1Ds Mark III, 5D, and 5D Mark II) because the image area for each of those cameras' sensors is larger than that of the Rebel T1i's sensor.

Note: While these EF-S lenses are designed specifically for EOS cameras with smaller image sensors, focal length is still focal length. It is incorrect to assume that the focal length labeled on the lens has been adjusted for smaller image sensors. This means that the 1.6x conversion factor still applies for the T1i.

Currently Canon has seven EF-S lenses. The EF-S 17-85mm f/4-5.6 IS USM is an image-stabilized zoom in a compact package. The EF-S 17-55 f/2.8 IS USM offers an image-stabilized zoom with a wide aperture. The EF-S 18-55mm f/3.5-5.6 IS is the kit lens that is often sold with the T1i.

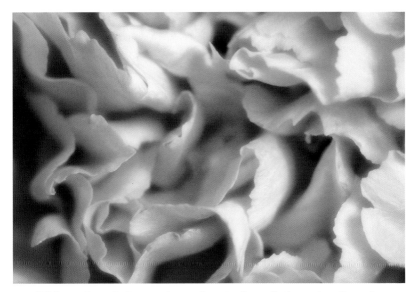

Wide-angle and close-up lenses have a dramatic impact on the subjects you normally shoot, as well as create uncommon and intriguing images.

The EF-S 10-22mm f/3.5-4.5 USM zoom brings an excellent wide-angle range to the Rebel T1i. For macro shooting Canon offers the EF-S 60mm f/2.8 Macro USM that focuses down to life-size magnification. On the opposite end of the lens spectrum is the EF-S 55-250mm f/4-5.6 IS which offers a very useful telephoto range. There is also the EF-S 18-200mm f/3.5-5.6 IS which gives you a bit more wide-angle shooting options, yet still offers telephoto.

Note: The EF-S series offers good value and great performance. The lenses make a great match for the T1i. Remember though, that if you see yourself stepping up to a full-frame sensor EOS camera, you will have to replace an EF-S lens—it will not work on a full-frame camera.

L-Series Lenses

Canon's L-series lenses use special optical technologies for high-quality lens correction, including low-dispersion glass, fluorite elements, and aspherical designs. UD (ultra-low dispersion) glass is used in telephoto lenses to minimize chromatic aberration, which occurs when the lens cannot focus all colors equally at the same point on the sensor (or on the film in a traditional camera), resulting in less sharpness and contrast. Low-dispersion glass focuses colors more equally for sharper, crisper images.

Fluorite elements are even more effective (though more expensive) and have the corrective power of two UD lens elements. Aspherical designs are used with wide-angle and mid-focal length lenses to correct the challenges of spherical aberration in such focal lengths. Spherical aberration is a problem caused by lens elements with extreme curvature (usually found in wide-angle and wide-angle zoom lenses). Glass tends to focus light differently through different parts of such a lens, causing a slight, overall softening of the image even though the lens is focused sharply. Aspherical lenses use a special design that compensates for this optical defect.

DO-Series Lenses

Another Canon optical design is the DO (diffractive optic). This technology significantly reduces the size and weight of a lens, and is therefore useful for big telephotos and zooms. Yet, the lens quality is unchanged. The lenses produced by Canon in this series are a 400mm pro lens that is only two-thirds the size and weight of the equivalent standard lens, and a 70-300mm IS lens that offers a great focal length range while including image stabilization.

Macro and Tilt-Shift Lenses

Canon also makes some specialized lenses. Macro lenses are single-focal-length lenses optimized for high sharpness throughout their focus range, from very close (1:1 or 1:2) magnifications to infinity. These lenses range from 50mm to 180mm.

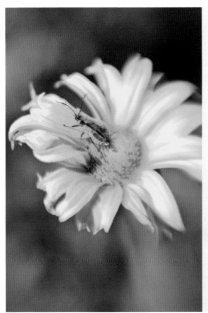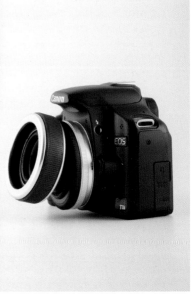

Lensbaby is an independent lens manufacturer that creates Canon-compatible lenses; these lenses create a selective focus effect.

Tilt-shift lenses are unique lenses that shift up and down or tilt toward or away from the subject. They mimic the controls of a view camera. Shift lets the photographer keep the back of the camera parallel to the scene and move the lens to get a tall subject into the composition. This keeps vertical lines vertical and is extremely valuable for architectural photographers. Tilt changes the plane of focus so that sharpness can be changed without changing the f/stop. Focus can be extended from near to far by tilting the lens toward the subject, or sharpness can be limited by tilting the lens away from the subject (which has been a trendy advertising photographic technique lately).

Independent Lens Brands

Independent lens manufacturers also make some excellent lenses that fit the Rebel T1i. I've seen quite a range in capabilities from these lenses. Some include low-dispersion glass and are stunningly sharp. Others may not match the best Canon lenses, but offer features (such as focal length range or a great price) that make them worth considering. To a degree, you get what you pay for. A low-priced Canon lens probably won't be much different than a low-priced independent lens. On the other hand, the high level of engineering and construction found on a Canon L-series lens can be difficult to match.

Filters

Many people assume that filters aren't needed for digital photography because adjustments for color and light can be made in the computer. By no means are filters obsolete! They actually save a substantial amount of work in the digital darkroom by allowing you to capture the desired color and tonalities for your image right from the start. Even if you can do certain things in the computer, why take the time if you can do them more efficiently while shooting?

Of course, the LCD monitor comes in handy once again. By using it, you can assist yourself in getting the best from your filters. If you aren't sure how a filter works, simply try it and see the results immediately on the monitor. This is like using a Polaroid, only better, because you need no extra gear. Just take the shot, review it, and make adjustments to the exposure or white balance to help the filter do its job. If a picture doesn't come out the way you would like, discard it and take another right away.

Attaching filters to the camera depends entirely on your lenses. Usually, a properly sized filter can either be screwed directly onto a lens, or fitted into a holder that screws onto the front of the lens. There are adapters to make a given size filter fit several lenses, but the filter must cover the lens from edge to edge or it will cause dark corners in the photo (vignetting). A photographer may even hold a filter over the lens with his or her hand.

There are a number of different types of filters that perform different tasks:

Polarizing Filters

This important outdoor filter should be in every camera bag. Its effects cannot be duplicated exactly with software because it actually affects the way light is perceived by the sensor.

A polarizer darkens skies—this effect is greatest when used at an angle that is 90° to the sun. As you move off this angle the effect diminishes. If your back is to the sun or you are shooting towards the direction of the sun, the polarizer will have no effect. A Polarizer can also reduce glare (which often makes colors look better), remove reflections, and increase saturation. While you can darken skies on the computer, the polarizer reduces the amount of work you have to perform in the digital darkroom. The filter can rotate in its mount, and as it rotates, the strength of the effect changes.

There are two types of polarizing filters, linear and circular. While linear polarizers often have the strongest effect, they can cause problems with exposure, and often prevent the camera from autofocusing. Consequently, you are safer using a circular polarizer with the Rebel T1i.

Neutral Density Gray Filters

Called ND filters, this type of filter is a helpful accessory. ND filters simply reduce the light coming through the lens. They are called neutral because they do not add any color tint to the scene. They come in different strengths, each reducing different quantities of light. They give additional exposure options under bright conditions, such as a beach or snow (where a filter with a strength of 4x is often appropriate). If you like the effects when slow shutter speeds are used with moving subjects like waterfalls, a strong neutral density filter (such as 8x) usually works well. Of course, the great advantage of the digital camera, again, is that you can see the effects of slow shutter speeds immediately on the LCD monitor so you can modify your exposure for the best possible effect.

Graduated Neutral Density Filters

Many photographers consider this filter an essential tool. It is half clear and half dark (gray). It is used to reduce bright areas (such as sky) in tone, while not affecting darker areas (such as the ground). The computer can mimic its effects, but you may not be able to recreate the scene you wanted. A digital camera's sensor can only respond to a certain range of brightness at any given exposure. If a part of the scene is too bright compared to the overall exposure, detail is washed out and no amount of work in the computer will bring it back. While you could try to capture two shots of the same scene at different exposure settings and then combine them on the computer, a graduated ND might be quicker.

UV and Skylight Filters

Most people use UV or skylight filters as protection for the front of their lens. Whether or not to use a "protective" filter on your lens is a never-ending debate. A lens hood/shade usually offers more protection than a glass filter and should be used at all times, even when the sun isn't out. Still, UV or skylight filters can be useful when photographing under such conditions as strong wind, rain, blowing sand, or going through brush.

If you use a filter for lens protection, a high-quality filter is best, as a cheap filter can degrade the optical quality of the lens. Remember that the manufacturer made the lens/sensor combination with very strict tolerances. A protective filter needs to be literally invisible, and only high-quality filters can guarantee that.

Close-Up Lenses

Close-up photography is a striking and unique way to capture a scene. Most of the photographs we see on a day-to-day basis are not close-ups, making those that do make their way to our eyes all the more noticeable. It is surprising to me that many photographers think the only way to shoot close-ups is with a macro lens. The following are four of the most common close-up options:

Close-focusing zoom lenses with a macro or close-focus feature: Most zoom lenses allow you to focus up-close without accessories, although focal-length choices may become limited when using the close-focus feature. These lenses are an easy and effective way to start shooting close-ups. Keep in mind, however, that even though these may say they have a macro setting, it is really just a close focus setting and not a true macro as described below in option four.

Close-up accessory lenses: You can buy lenses that screw onto the front of your lens to allow it to focus even closer. The advantage is that you now have the whole range of zoom focal lengths available and there are no exposure corrections. Close-up filters can do this, but the image quality is not great. More expensive achromatic accessory lenses (highly-corrected, multi-element lenses) do a superb job with close-up work, but their quality is limited by the original lens.

Extension tubes: Extension tubes fit in between the lens and the camera body of an SLR. This allows the lens to focus much closer than it could normally do so. Extension tubes are designed to work with all lenses for your camera (although older extension tubes won't always match some of the new lenses made specifically for digital cameras). Be aware that extension tubes cause a loss of light.

Macro lenses: Though relatively expensive, macro lenses are designed for superb sharpness at all distances and focus from mere inches to infinity. In addition, they are typically very sharp at all f/stops.

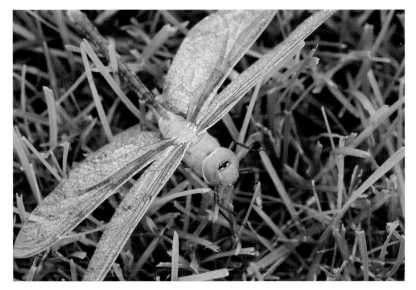

Close-up lenses allow you to get your camera physically closer to your subject for tighter, more controlled compositions.

Close-up Sharpness

Sharpness is a big issue with close-ups, and this is not simply a matter of buying a well-designed macro lens. The other close-up options can also give superbly sharp images. Sharpness problems usually result from three factors: limited depth of field, incorrect focus placement, and camera movement.

The closer you get to a subject, the shallower depth of field becomes. You can stop your lens down as far as it will go for more depth of field. Because of this, it is critical to be sure focus is placed correctly on the subject. If the back of an insect is sharp but its eyes aren't, the photo appears to have a focus problem. At these close distances, every detail counts. If only half of the flower petals are in focus, the overall photo does not look sharp. Autofocus up close can be a real problem with critical focus placement because the camera often focuses on the wrong part of the photo.

Of course, you can review your photo on the LCD monitor to be sure the focus is correct before leaving your subject. You can also try manual focus. One technique is to focus the lens at a reasonable distance, then move the camera toward and away from the subject as you watch it go in and out of focus. This can really help, but still, you may find that taking multiple photos is the best way to guarantee proper focus at these close distances. Another good technique is to shoot using the ⬚ drive mode and fire multiple photos. You may find at least one shot with the critical part of your subject in focus. This is a great technique when you are handholding and when you want to capture moving subjects.

When you are focusing close, even slight movement can shift the camera dramatically in relationship to the subject. The way to help correct this is to use a high shutter speed or put the camera on a tripod. Two advantages to using a digital camera during close-up work are the ability to check the image to see if you are having camera movement problems, and the ability to change ISO settings from picture to picture (enabling a faster shutter speed if you deem it necessary).

Close-Up Contrast
The best looking close-up images are often ones that allow the subject to contrast with its background, making it stand out and adding some drama to the photo. Although maximizing contrast is important in any photograph where you want to emphasize the subject, it is particularly critical for close-up subjects where a slight movement of the camera can totally change the background.

There are three important contrast options to keep in mind:

Tonal or brightness contrasts: Look for a background that is darker or lighter than your close-up subject. This may mean a small adjustment in camera position. Backlight is excellent for this since it offers bright edges on your subject with lots of dark shadows behind it.

Color contrasts: Color contrast is a great way to make your subject stand out from the background. Flowers are popular close-up subjects and, with their bright colors, they are perfect candidates for this type of contrast. Just look for a background that is either a completely different color (such as green grass behind red flowers) or a different saturation of color (such as a bright green bug against dark green grass).

Sharpness contrast: One of the best close-up techniques is to work with the inherent limit in depth of field and deliberately set a sharp subject against an out-of-focus background or foreground. Look at the distance between your subject and its surroundings. How close are other objects to your subject? Move to a different angle so that distractions do not conflict with the edges of your subject. Try different f/stops to change the look of an out-of-focus background or foreground.

Tripods and Camera Support

A successful approach to getting the most from a digital camera is to be aware that camera movement can affect sharpness and tonal brilliance in an image. Even slight movement during the exposure can cause the loss of fine details and the blurring of highlights. These effects are especially glaring when you compare an affected image to a photo that has no motion problems. In addition, affected images do not enlarge well.

You must minimize camera movement in order to maximize the capabilities of your lens and sensor. A steady hold on the camera is a start. Fast shutter speeds, as well as the use of flash, help to ensure sharp photos, although you can get away with slower shutter speeds when using wider-angle lenses. When shutter speeds go down, however, it is advisable to use a camera-stabilizing device. Tripods, beanbags, monopods, mini-tripods, shoulder stocks, clamps, and more, all help. Many photographers carry a small beanbag or a clamp pod with their camera equipment for those situations where the camera needs support but a tripod isn't available.

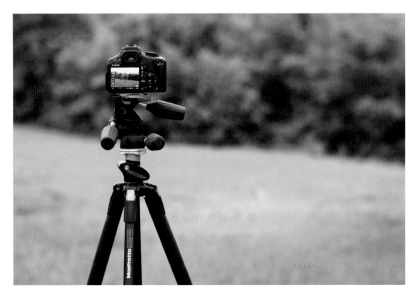

Regardless of what lens you use, a tripod will ensure you maximize the len's ability to achieve the highest quality image possible.

Check your local camera store for a variety of stabilizing equipment. A good tripod is an excellent investment and it will last through many different camera upgrades. When buying one, extend it all the way to see how easy it is to open, then lean on it to see how stiff it is. Both aluminum and carbon fiber tripods offer great rigidity. Carbon fiber is much lighter, but also more expensive. A new option that is in the middle in price/performance between aluminum and carbon fiber is basalt. Basalt tripods are stronger than aluminum but not quite as light as carbon fiber.

The tripod head is a very important part of the tripod and may be sold separately. There are two basic types for still photography: the ball head and the pan-and-tilt head. Both designs are capable of solid support and both have their passionate advocates. The biggest difference between them is how you loosen the controls and adjust the camera. Try both

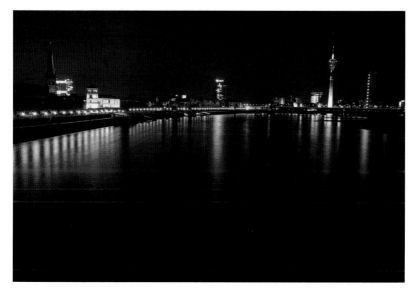

Tripods are an important tool for low-light shooting, and they are a must for nighttime shots, such as this cityscape.

and see which seems to work better for you. Be sure to do this with a camera on the tripod because that added weight changes how the head works. Make sure that the tripod and head you choose can properly support the weight of the T1i and all the lenses you will be using.

When shooting video, it often necessary to pan the camera left or right or tilt the camera up and down to follow action. Some "photo" heads allow panning, but many might not have a panning handle that allows you to operate the head while looking at the LCD monitor. If your tripod head allows panning, it may not have the ability to tilt smoothly while recording video. Consider adding a video head to your tripod. Look for a "fluid" video head that will offer smooth movement in all directions. Once again, make sure that the head is the right size for the T1i and the lenses and lens accessories that you plan to use.

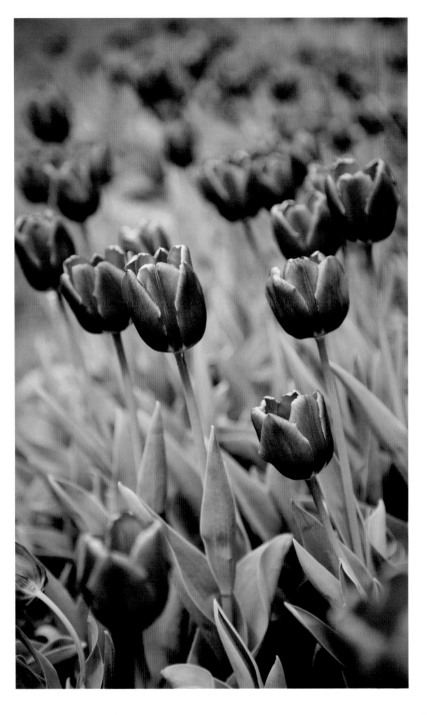

Camera to Computer

One you have captured your images and movies, you need to move them to your computer. There are two main ways of transferring digital files from the memory card. One way is to insert the card into an accessory known as a media card reader. Card readers connect to your computer through the USB or FireWire port and can remain plugged in and ready to download your images or videos. The second way is to download images directly from the T1i using a USB interface cable (included with the camera at the time of purchase).

FireWire (also called iLink or 1394) is faster than USB but might not be standard on your computer. There are several types of USB: USB 1.0, 2.0, and 2.0 Hi-Speed. Older computers and card readers will have the 1.0 version, but new devices are most likely 2.0 Hi-Speed. This new version of USB is much faster than the old. However, if you have both versions of USB devices plugged into the same bus, the older devices will slow down the faster devices.

The advantage of downloading directly from the camera is that you don't need to buy a card reader. However, there are some distinct disadvantages. For one, cameras generally download much more slowly than card readers (given the same connections). Plus, a camera has to be unplugged from the computer after each use, while the card reader can be left attached. In addition to these drawbacks, downloading directly from a camera uses its battery power (and shortens battery life by using up charge cycles) in making the transfer (or you need to plug it into AC power).

↶ *A card reader is often the more preferred method of transferring images from the memory card to the computer, especially when transferring the Rebel T1i's hi-definition video files.*

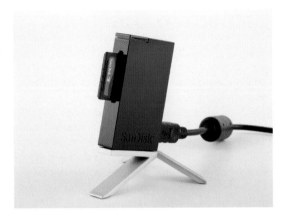

A card reader saves on wear and tear on your camera's battery. Make sure your reader can handle SDHC cards.

The Card Reader

A card reader can be purchased at most camera or electronics stores. There are several different types, including single-card readers that read only one particular type of memory card, or multi-readers that are able to utilize several different kinds of cards. (The latter are important with the Rebel T1i only if you have several cameras using different memory card types.)

Note: If you are going to use SDHC memory cards (as I recommend), you must use a card reader that supports SDHC. Just because the card fits into an SD slot does not mean it will work. See page 55 to learn more about SDHC.

After your card reader is connected to your computer, remove the memory card from your camera and put it into the appropriate slot in your card reader.

The card usually appears as an additional drive on your computer (on Windows Vista or XP and Mac OS X operating systems—for other versions you may have to install the drivers that come with the card reader). When the computer recognizes the card, it may also give instructions for downloading. Follow these instructions if you are unsure about opening and moving the files yourself, or simply select your files and drag them to the folder or drive where you want them (a much faster approach). Make sure you "eject" the card before removing it from the reader. On Windows you right click on the drive and select eject; on a Mac, you drag the memory card icon to the trash.

Card readers can also be used with laptops, though PC card adapters may be more convenient when you're on the move. As long as your laptop has a PC card slot, all you need is a PC card adapter for SDHC memory cards. Insert the memory card into the PC adapter, and then insert the PC adapter into your laptop's PC card slot. Once the computer recognizes this as a new drive, drag and drop images from the card to the hard drive. The latest PC card adapter models tend to be faster—but are also more expensive—than card readers.

Archiving

Without proper care, your digital images and movies can be lost or destroyed. Many photographers back up their files with a second drive, either added to the inside of the computer or as an external USB or FireWire drive. This is a popular and somewhat cost-effective method of safeguarding your data.

Hard drives and memory cards do a great job at recording image files and movie clips for processing, transmitting, and sharing, but are not great for long-term storage. Hard drives are designed to spin; just sitting on a shelf can cause problems. This type of media has been known to lose data within ten years. And since drives and cards are getting progressively larger, the chance that a failure will wipe out thousands of images and movies rather than "just one roll of shots or tape" is always increasing. Computer viruses or power surges can also wipe out files from a hard drive. Even the best drives can crash, rendering them unusable. Plus, we are all capable of accidentally erasing or saving over an important photo or movie. Consider using redundant drives for critical data backup.

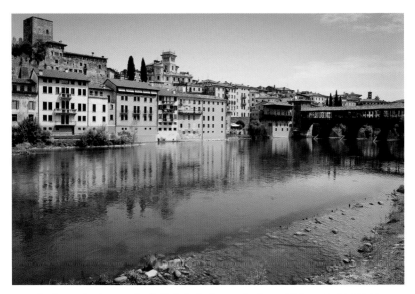

An important aspect of digital photography is archiving your images properly. Optical media such as DVD and Blu-ray discs have taken the place of film negatives, but there are many other storage options available.

For more permanent backup, burn your files to optical discs: CD or DVD (recommended). A CD-writer (or "burner") used to be the standard for the digital photographer, but image files are getting too big and high definition movie files are just about out of the question. DVDs can handle about seven times the data that can be saved on a CD, but even standard DVDs are becoming inconvenient for larger file sizes. Blu-ray discs (see below) may be the solution.

There are two types of DVDs (and CDs) that can be used for recording data: R designated (i.e. DVD-R) recordable discs; and RW designated (i.e. DVD-RW) rewritable discs. DVD-R discs can only be recorded once—they cannot be erased. DVD-RWs, on the other hand, can be recorded on, erased, and then reused later. If you want long-term storage of your images, use -R discs rather than -RWs. (The latter are best used for temporary storage, such as transporting images to a new location.) The storage medium used for -R discs is more stable than that of -RWs (which makes a little sense since the DVD-RWs are designed to be erasable).

As mentioned above, a new format, Blu-ray, is starting to be an option. This system uses a different colored laser (blue-violet) to read data. The use of a higher frequency light source means more data can be written to the disc. A single layer Blu-ray disc can hold about 25GB of data, which is more than 5 times as much data as a single layer DVD. A dual layer Blu-ray disc can hold 50GB. This technology is quite new, however, so be aware that there may be some growing pains. As with DVDs and CDs there are write-once (BD-R) and eraseable (BD-RE) discs. Stick to BD-R for archive reliability.

Optical discs take the place of negatives in the digital world. Set up a DVD binder for your digital "negatives". You may want to keep your original and edited images on separate discs (or separate folders on the same disc).

As mentioned above, stay away from optical media that is rewriteable like DVD-RW or for Blu-ray, BD-RE. You want the most reliable archive. At this point rewritable discs, while convenient, are not as reliable for archiving. Also avoid any options that let you create multiple "sessions" on the disc. This feature allows you to add more data to the disc until it is full. For the highest reliability, write all of the data to the disc at once.

Buy quality media. Inexpensive discs may not preserve your photo-image files as long as you would like them to. Read the box. Look for information about the life of the disc. Most long-lived discs are labeled as such and cost a little more. And once you have written to the disc, store and handle it properly.

Working with Still Images

How do you edit and file your digital photos so they are accessible and easy to use? To start, it helps to create folders specific to groups of images (i.e., Outdoors, Sports, State Fair, Furniture Displays, etc.). You can organize your folders alphabetically or by date inside a "parent" folder. The organization and processing of images is called workflow. (If you want to start a heated conversation among digital photographers, ask them about workflow!)

Note: Even though the T1i puts both image and movie files into the same folder on the memory card, it is a good idea to divide the files by type and put them in separate folders. This will help when you use the separate image editing and video editing applications.

Be sure to edit your stills to remove extraneous shots. Unwanted files stored on your computer waste storage space on your hard drive. They also increase the time you must spend when you browse through your images, so store only the ones you intend to keep. Take a moment to review your files while the card is still in the camera. Erase the ones you don't want, and download the rest. You can also delete files once they are downloaded to the computer by using a browser program (described below).

Here's how I deal with digital still files. (Later in this chapter I cover movies.) First, I set up an image filing system. I use a folder called Digital Images. Inside Digital Images I have folders by year, and within those, the individual shoots (you could use locations, clients, whatever works for you). This is really no different than setting up an office filing cabinet with hanging folders or envelopes to hold photos. Consider the Digital Images folder to be the file cabinet, and the individual folders inside to be the equivalent of the file cabinet's hanging folders.

Next, I use a memory card reader that shows up as a drive on my computer. Using the computer's file system, I open the memory card as a window or open folder (this is the same basic view on both Windows and Mac computers) showing the images in the appropriate folder. I then open another window or folder on the computer's hard drive and navigate to the Digital Images folder, then to the year folder. I create a new subfolder labeled to signify the photographs on the memory card, such as Place, Topic, Date.

Then, I select all the images (no movies) in the memory card folder and drag them to the new folder on my hard drive. This copies all the images onto the hard drive and into my "filing cabinet". It is actually better than using a physical filing cabinet because, for example, I can use browser software to rename all the photos in the new folder, giving information about each photo, for example using the title DeathValleyMay09.

I also set up a group of folders in a separate "filing cabinet" (a new folder at the level of Digital Images) for edited photos. In this second filing cabinet, I include subfolders specific to types of photography, such as landscapes, close-ups, people, etc. Within these subfolders, I can break down categories even further when that helps to organize my photos. Inside the subfolders I place copies of original images that I have examined and decided are definite keepers, both unprocessed (direct from the camera) and processed images (keeping such files separate). Make sure these are copies (don't just move the files here), as it is important to keep all "original" photo files in the original folder that they went to when first downloaded.

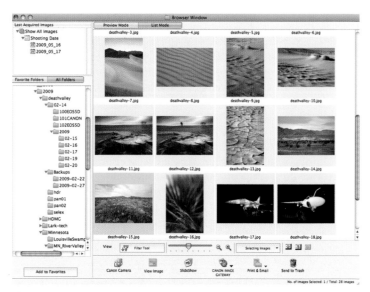

Canon's ImageBrowser is useful for cataloging your images. In addition, it can use it to open images into Digital Photo Professional.

Image Browser Programs

Image browser programs allow you to quickly look at photos on your computer, rename them one at a time or all at once, read all major files, move photos from folder to folder, resize photos for e-mailing, create simple slideshows, and more. Some are good at image editing and some are not.

One of the most popular names in image editing is Adobe and their flagship application is Adobe Photoshop. While the CS4 version of Adobe Photoshop has an improved Bridge that can help organize photos, there are currently a number of other programs that help you view and organize your images.

ACDSee is a superb program with a customizable interface and an easy-to-use keyboard method of rating of images. It also has some unique characteristics, such as a calendar feature that lets you find photos by date (though the best-featured version is Windows only). Another very good program with similar capabilities is Microsoft's Expression Media (with equal features on both Windows and Mac versions).

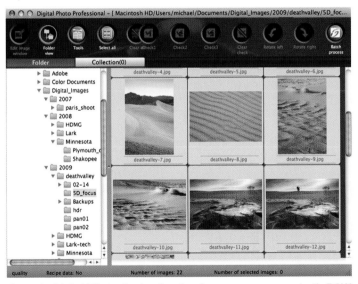

Canon's Digital Photo Professional software can process both RAW and JPEG images.

Apple's Aperture uses a digital "loupe" to magnify your images while browsing (it is only available for the Mac). It is more than just a browser in that it offers full image editing too. Check out Canon's Digital Photo Professional, included with the software that comes with the T1i. It is the only software that is able to utilize Canon's Dust Delete Detect system.

Adobe's Lightroom is also an option. Although its official name is Photoshop Lightroom, I like to leave off Photoshop because it can intimidate photographers. Like Aperture, Lightroom is more than just a browser. It has full image processing tools and tools for printing pictures, making slide shows and building web pages. The concept behind Lightroom (and Aperture) is to build an application that is specifically designed for photographers, rather than a program that has a lot of tools for other uses.

There is also Adobe's light version of Photoshop, called Photoshop Elements. Calling it light is a misnomer because it contains a lot of the functionality of Photoshop, but is less intimidating.

All of these programs include some database functions (such as keyword searches) and many operate on both Windows and Mac platforms.

An important function of browser programs is their ability to print customized index prints. You can then give a title to each of the index prints and list additional information about the photographer, as well as the photos' file location. The index print is a hard copy that allows easy reference (and visual searches). If you include an index print with every DVD you burn, you can quickly see what is on the DVD and find the file you need. A combination of uniquely labeled file folders on your hard drive, a browser program, and index prints help you maintain a fast and easy way to find and sort images.

Image Processing

Once the files – JPEG or RAW – are organized on your computer, you must consider image processing. Of course, you can process the T1i's JPEG files in any image-processing program. One nice thing about JPEG is that it is one of the most universally recognized formats. Any program on any computer that recognizes image files will recognize JPEG. That

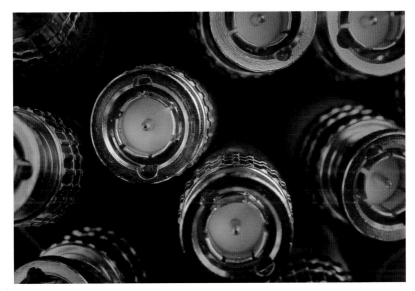

Image processing has become almost as important as shooting the image itself. RAW files allow an immense amount of creative control, but require post-processing in order to be viewed in a final form, such as online or as a print.

said, it is important to understand that the original JPEG file is more like a negative than a slide. Sure, you can use it directly, just like you could have the local mini-lab make prints from negatives. But JPEG files can be processed to get more out of them.

RAW is an important format because it increases the options for adjustment of your images. In addition, Canon's RAW file, CR2, offers increased flexibility and control over the image. But when you shoot RAW, you have to "process" every image so they won't look dull and lifeless. This changes your workflow. This is why photographers who sometimes, but not always, need to work with RAW will use the T1i's ability to record RAW and JPEG at the same time.

A big advantage to the T1i RAW file is that it captures more directly what the sensor sees. It holds more information

(14 bits vs. the standard 8 bits per color) and stronger correction can be applied to it (compared to JPEG images) before artifacts appear. This can be particularly helpful when there are difficulties with exposure or color balance. (Keep in mind that the image file from the camera holds 14 bits of data even though it is contained in a 16-bit file—so while you can get a 16-bit TIFF file from the RAW file, it is based on 14 bits of data.)

While RAW files offer more capacity for change, you can still do a lot with a JPEG file to optimize it for use. I shoot a lot of JPEG when it fits my workflow, and no one complains about the quality of my images.

Note: EOS T1i RAW files are about 20MB in size so they fill memory cards quite quickly. With larger file sizes come increases in processing and workflow times.

Canon offers two ways to convert CR2 files to standard files that can be optimized in an image editor like Photoshop: a file viewer utility (ZoomBrowser EX for Windows or ImageBrowser for Mac) and the Digital Photo Professional software. In addition, Photoshop, Lightroom, Aperture, and Capture One have RAW processing built-in. Each application has its own RAW processing engine that interprets the images, so there is a slight difference between programs in the final result.

Note: If you have an older version of any of these programs, you probably need to update your software in order to open the latest version of the RAW CR2 files. Unfortunately, the older versions of some image editing applications are no longer updated to handle the new RAW files of the T1i.

The File Viewer Utility

Canon's ZoomBrowser EX (Windows)/ImageBrowser (Mac) supplied with the camera is easy to use. It is a good "browser" program that lets you view and organize RAW and JPEG files. It will convert RAW files, though it is a pretty basic program and doesn't offer some of the features available in other RAW processing software. Even so, it does a very good job of translating details from the RAW file into TIFF, PICT, BMP, or JPEG form. Once converted, any image-processing program can read the new TIFF or JPEG. TIFF is the preferred file format because it is uncompressed; JPEG should only be used if you have file space limitations. You can also use the software to create an image suitable for email, print images and even present a quick slide show of selected images. The image browsers supplied with the T1i are much faster than earlier versions.

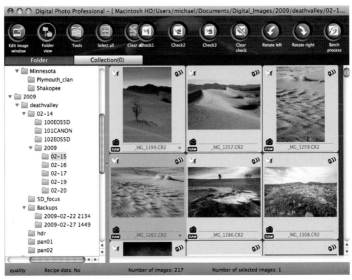

Canon's Digital Photo Professional software is the only way to make use of the Dust Delete Detection data embedded into each T1i image file.

Digital Photo Professional Software

This is Canon's advanced proprietary program for processing RAW and JPEG images. Once an optional program and now included with the T1i, Digital Photo Professional (DPP) was developed to bring Canon RAW file processing up to speed with the rest of the digital world. This program has a powerful processing engine. It can be used to process both CR2 files and JPEG files. The advantage to processing JPEG files is that DPP is quicker and easier to use than Photoshop, yet is still quite powerful. For fast and simple JPEG processing, DPP works quite well.

I believe if you are going to shoot RAW, DPP is a must-use program. It is fast, full-featured and gives excellent results. One big advantage that DPP offers over any other RAW processing program is the ability to use Dust Delete Detection Data that is embedded in the RAW file. It can also read the aspect ratio information embedded in the image files so it can crop images automatically.

The remote control screen of EOS Utility allows you to control most shooting functions of the T1i when connected to a computer via the USB cable.

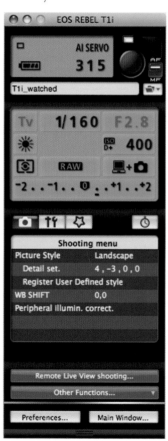

EOS Utility

This application serves as a gateway for several operations with the T1i and accessories. First, it is used to download images (all images or just those selected) when the camera is connected via USB to the computer.

EOS Utility is also used for remote or "tethered" shooting. When you start up this feature, you can fire the shutter, choose exposure mode, and adjust shutter speed, aperture, ISO, white balance, metering mode, and file recording type. There is limited access to menus: you can set Picture

Style, personal white balance, JPEG quality, and white balance shift in the Shooting menu displayed on the computer. In the Setup menu on the computer you can give the camera an owner's name, change the date and time, enable Live View, and update the firmware.

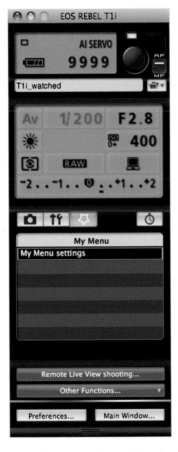

While you might think of EOS Utility as strictly a tethered shooting device, it also a great tool for easily setting up your My Menu.

Access to the My Menu setup while tethered is a fast way to set up your My Menu. Even if you never "shoot" tethered, consider hooking up the camera to set up the My Menu. Instead of scrolling through seemingly endless options on the small T1i LCD monitor, use the remote camera control to point and click your way through choices.

While tethered, you can turn on Live View shooting for a powerful studio-style, image-preview shooting setup. An instant histogram and the ability to check focus help during tethered Live View. You have the choice of capturing the images to the computer, or to the computer and the memory card in the T1i. As you capture each picture, it can open automatically in Digital Photo Professional or in the image editor of your choice.

EOS Utility also offers the option of timed shooting. The computer acts as an intervalometer, taking a picture every few seconds (from 5 seconds to 99 hours and 59 seconds). You can also do a bulb exposure from 5 seconds to 99 hours and 59 seconds. In most cases Live View shooting, timed or bulb, will require the computer and camera to operate off AC power.

Note: The T1i supports embedding copyright information in the metadata of your images. Your name and a year and any other text can be added to this metadata field. The only way to enter this data is using EOS Utility.

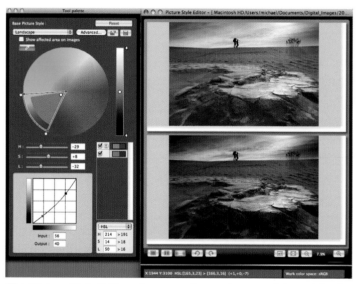

The Picture Style Editor allows you to create new picture styles by using a visual interface. You get instant feedback on an actual image while making adjustments.

Picture Style Editor

The Picture Style Editor lets you create your own styles. When you import a RAW image, you are able to adjust its overall tone curve much as you would in an image editor. You can also adjust the normal picture style parameters of sharpness, contrast, color saturation, and color tone.

But the Picture Style Editor's most powerful feature is the ability to change individual colors in the image. Use an eye-dropper tool to pick a color and then adjust the hue, saturation and luminance values of the color. You can pick multiple colors and also choose how wide or how narrow a range of colors (around the selected color) are adjusted. These custom picture styles can then be uploaded to the T1i using EOS Utility. You can also download new picture styles that have been created by Canon engineers at:
http://www.usa.canon.com/content/picturestyle/file/index.html

Direct Printing

If you use certain compatible Canon printers, you can control printing directly from the T1i. Simply connect the camera to the printer using the dedicated USB cord that comes with the T1i. Compatible Canon printers provide access to many direct printing features, including:

• Contact sheet style 35-image index prints
• Print date and filename
• Print shooting information
• Face brightening
• Red-eye reduction
• Print sizes (printer dependent), including 4 x 6, 5 x 7, 8.5 x 11
• Support for other paper types
• Print effects and image optimization: Natural, Vivid, B/W, Cool Tone, Warm Tone, Noise Reduction

Note: Because of the wide variety of printers, it is possible not all the printing features mentioned in this chapter are on your printer. For a detailed list of options available when the T1i is connected to your Canon printer, consult your printer's manual.

The T1i is PictBridge compatible, meaning that it can be connected directly to PictBridge printers from several manufacturers. Most new photo printers are PictBridge

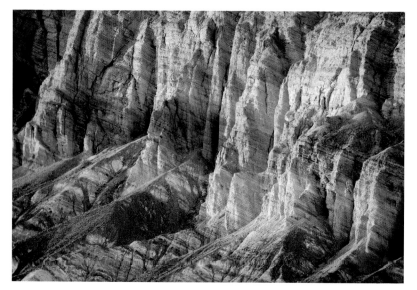

Unlike older Digital Rebels, the T1i allows you to print RAW files on a PictBridge printer.

compatible. When you use a PictBridge printer, use the USB cord that comes with the camera. (More information on Pict-Bridge can be found at: www.canon.com/pictbridge/.)

Note: Both RAW and JPEG files can be used for the direct printing options mentioned in this section, but movies cannot be printed.

To start the printing process, first make sure that both the camera and the printer are turned off. Connect the camera to the printer with the camera's USB cord (the connections are straightforward since the plugs only work one way). Turn on the printer first, then the camera—this lets the camera recognize the printer so it is prepared to control it. (Some printers may turn on automatically when the power cable is connected.) Depending on the printer, the camera's direct printing features may vary.

Press Playback ▶ and ◻/⊡∿ will light up to indicate that the camera is successfully connected to the printer. ⚡ in the upper left of the LCD also indicates the printer is connected. Use ◀▶ to select an image on the LCD monitor that you want to print. Press ⊛ and the Print Setting screen appears, listing such printing choices as image optimization, whether to imprint the date, the number of copies, trimming area, and paper settings (size, type, borders, or borderless).

Trimming is a great choice because it allows you to crop your photo right in the LCD monitor before printing, tightening up the composition if needed. To trim, first use ▲▼ to select [Trimming] and press ⊛. Use ⊕ and ⊡·⊖ to adjust the size of the crop; use ✧ to adjust the position of the crop. Use DISP. to rotate the crop 90° and ⌂ to rotate the image within the crop. Press ⊛ to accept the crop setting.

Note: Depending on the printer, trimming and printing the date may not be available.

Depending on your printer, you can also adjust print effects to print images in black and white—in a neutral tone, cool tone or warm tone. Other effects include noise reduction, face brightening and red-eye correction. You can also choose to use a natural or vivid color setting. Some printers may not support all effects.

Continue using ✧ to select other settings. These choices may change, depending on the printer; refer to the printer's manual if necessary.

Once you have selected the options you want, then use ✧ to select [Print] and press ⊛ to start printing. The LCD monitor confirms that the image is being printed and reminds you not to disconnect the cable during the printing process. Wait for that message to disappear before disconnecting the camera from the printer. If you wish to use the same settings for additional prints, use ✧ to move to the next picture, then simply press ⊛ to print the next image.

Note: The amount of control you have over the image when you print directly from the camera is limited solely by the printer. If you need more image control, print from the computer.

If you shoot a lot of images for direct printing, do some test shots and set up the T1i's Picture Styles (see page 93) to optimize the prints before shooting the final pictures. You may even want to create a custom setting that increases sharpness and saturation just for this purpose.

Digital Print Order Format (DPOF)

Another of the T1i's printing features is DPOF (Digital Print Order Format) ♪. This allows you to decide which images to print before you actually do any printing. Then, if you use a printer that recognizes DPOF, the printer automatically prints just the images you have chosen. DPOF is also a way to select images on a memory card for printing at a photo lab. After the images on your SD/SDHC card are selected using DPOF, drop it off at the photo lab—assuming their equipment recognizes DPOF (ask before you leave your card)—and they will know which prints you want.

DPOF is accessible through the Playback 1 menu ▣ under [Print order]. You can choose several options: Select [Set Up] to choose Print type (Standard, Index, or Both), Date (On or Off), and File No. (On or Off). Once you set your print options, press **MENU** to return to [Print order]. From there you have two ways to select images to print: Select [All image] or select images manually. To select images manually, highlight [Sel Image], press ⊜ and then use ✧ to scroll through your images. Press ▲ WB to set the number of copies to print for the current image. If you are printing an index print, use ⊜ to select an image to include on the index print. You can also press ▣·⊙ to bring up a three-image display to select images. Use ◄► and ▲ WB to go through and mark all of the images to be printed. Press **MENU** to return to the [Print order] screen. The total number of prints ordered appears on the screen.

Note: RAW and movie files cannot be selected for DPOF printing. If you shoot RAW+JPEG, then you can use DPOF. The JPEG versions of the files will be printed.

If you are printing the images yourself, once you have selected all the images, connect the camera to the printer. A Print button appears on the Print Order screen. Use ✧ to highlight, and then press ⊛. Set up image optimization and paper settings, then select [OK] and press ⊛ to start the printing process. If you are using a photofinisher for DPOF, make sure that you back up your memory card and that the photofinisher supports DPOF.

Working with Movies

Workflow for movies is different from that used for still images. File sizes can be extremely large and some editing programs work best if the files are in the right place. Generally movie clips need to be edited together opposed to a single image that may stand alone as a single photograph. In other words, video clips are often "program" based; a single clip won't have the impact that a single photograph does. In addition, video may be scripted or storyboarded.

My workflow for video is very much project-based. It also requires a concerted effort to think about archiving even before I start editing the project. Once I have finished recording, I create a project folder on a high-speed external drive. Depending on the size of the drive, that folder might be in a folder that includes the year or the month so I can keep projects separate. For example, I might have a structure of 2009/May/Wildcat_Sanctuary/. Once the file structure is in place, I copy my footage into the new folder.

Depending on the software application I choose for video editing, I may then view each file and rename the files. If I were doing interviews, I would rename the file with the person's last name and then a take number, such as Ally01, Ally02, etc. If I use an editing application like Final Cut Pro,

I might leave the file name alone and do all of the descriptive data entry in the editing program.

The nice part about changing the name at the file level is that it is more descriptive. You can search within the file system, rather than opening up an editing application. On the other hand, the advantage of changing the name in the editing program is that you can use longer names and you can include information like take number, comments, camera angle, script notes, whether a clip is good or bad, etc., in columns next to the file name (depending on your editing software).

Note: Once you bring the files into your editor and you start to edit, don't use the file system to change the file names of the movies. The files may become unlinked from your project. Also, don't move them from the folders that they are in, as this could break the link too. Although there are ways to relink files, they don't always work.

Once I have the file names set, I copy the folder to my archive drive, or—if the folder is small enough—an optical disc (Blu-ray). (See Archiving, above.) This way I have a working copy on the high-speed drive and an untouched copy for archive. When you edit video, you don't change pixels on the original files; to revise a project, all you need is the project file and the original movies the project is linked to.

Viewing Movies

Canon's ZoomBrowser EX (Windows)/ImageBrowser (Mac), supplied with the T1i, can play back individual movie clips, trim them and even save a still frame, but you can't edit the clips into a sequence. If you merely want to view your files, QuickTime player is a good (and free!) application. The Pro version of QuickTime lets you trim clips and even build a rough sequence, but it is not very intuitive and does not foster a lot of creativity. For that, you need a real editing application.

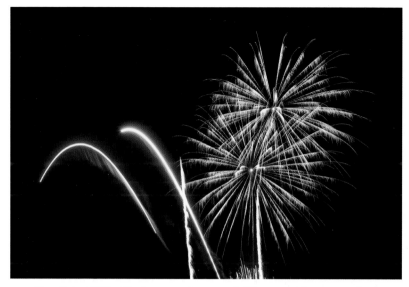

The Rebel T1i's Movie recording capabilities provide an excellent chance to experiment with long shots and short films, and allow you to take still images while recording video.

Note: If you are on the Windows platform you may need to install QuickTime in order to view your movie clips. Download the Windows version at www.apple.com/quicktime/. For simple playback of movies, it is not necessary to buy the QuickTime Pro version or download iTunes with QuickTime. Download just the "plain" version of QuickTime.

Movie Editing

There is quite an assortment of video editing applications for both Windows and Mac computer platforms and for all budgets. On the Windows side, there is Adobe Premiere and Premiere Elements, Sony Vegas, Pinnacle Studio, Corel VideoStudio X2. For Mac users, there is Adobe Premiere, Avid's Media Composer and Xpress Pro, Media 100, and Apple's iMovie, Final Cut Express, and Final Cut Studio.

Costs for the software alone range from "included with your computer" to nearly $2,500. If you do simple cuts and dissolves and not much in the way of effects, layering or complicated projects, the less expensive options can work. The more expensive applications give you more options for the output of your finished project—compression for the web or authoring Blu-ray discs.

Manipulating HD video is very taxing on a computer. These are essentially large image files that are flying by at 20 or 30 frames a second, so you need a computer that can handle it. Bulk up on RAM and processor speed—as much as you can afford.

Several of the editing applications—Premiere and Final Cut Pro, for example—can edit natively (without having to convert to another file format) in the h.264 codec. The h.264 is a highly efficient algorithm. It reduces both file size and the data rate needed to record the movie. Unfortunately, it takes a great deal of computing power to make this happen. You may find that your computer, which worked fine running Photoshop and editing RAW files, can struggle just to play back a single movie file without stuttering frames. Generally this is caused either by a slow disc drive or by a slow processor (CPU).

Will editing natively in the h.264 code work for you? It all depends on the application you are using, your computer's horsepower and your tolerance for the process. I have edited with h.264 on a laptop in a hotel room, where I could only play the original files without jerkiness. The minute I put the clips into a sequence, the computer couldn't keep up. Fortunately, my editing experience helped me mark "in" and "out" times for each clip and I instinctively knew how the sequence would play. I checked my edited program afterwards when I exported the sequence—a process that took over half an hour. In this instance I could tolerate the slow times and uncertainty because I needed to travel light. But that's me; how you tolerate that kind of workflow could be very different.

Since h.264 is not really optimized as an editing format, there are several workarounds to overcome the need for the fastest computer and the most RAM. One method is to "transcode" the file to another codec. "Transcoding a file" means making a copy and recompressing it. If your computer is slowing down, try a codec that is uncompressed or one that is more suitable for editing (like XDCAM-HD or Apple's ProRes). One problem with transcoding is that the color space or dynamic range might change; some highlights might change; detail could disappear; and/or colors might shift. Make sure you compare the transcoded file to the original. Another issue may be rendering times if you need to output back to an h.264 file. If this is the case, you should perform some test renders so you know how long it will take. You don't want to be surprised if your final project takes 3 hours to render, especially if it was supposed to be completed an hour ago.

Another option to reduce processor load is to edit in a low-resolution proxy mode. Proxies are to movies, what thumbnails are to photos. They are low-resolution video clips. This is the technique that Corel Video Studio Pro X2 uses. It converts the high-definition movies to smaller movies that are easier to use during the editing process. Once the edit is complete, the software links up to the original high-definition files for output.

Movie Output

When you have finished editing, you'll have to output the movie. It is important to consider this process before you begin editing. When you work with still images, you have fewer output options: prints or digital files for computer display. (Of course there are others but these two are the usual ones.) When you work with movies, it may appear there are only a few options, but they can quickly multiply.

For example, say you are asked to deliver to a web site. Once you start asking questions, you'll be surprised at the complexity. First, there is window size: most places can't take the full 1920x1080 or 1280x720 or even 640x480 file,

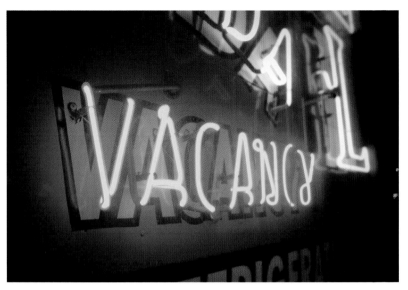

1920x1080 or 1280x720 are both wide screen high definition formats. The former records at 20 frames per second, the latter at 30 frames per second.

and may ask for 1/2 size or 1/4 size. Then there is the file type: Do they want h.264, Windows Media (.wmv), Flash, Quicktime? How about the file size? This is not the same as the window size. Internet delivery is highly dependent on connection bandwidth and the amount of compression you apply to a movie directly affects how much bandwidth is needed. Finally there is frame rate. Some sites can play back a 30-frame-per-second movie; others require half that rate.

Note: There isn't one "best" solution. Each website or host has its own requirements that, unfortunately, may constantly change. It is important that you do your research before you start shooting, so you know what you need to deliver. In fact, you may need to deliver multiple versions of the file.

If you want to deliver high definition on optical disc, there are two options. First, you can compress your finished program into a codec that is supported on Blu-ray. You then author a Blu-ray disc that can play on a set top Blu-ray player. Many of the applications above can do this, or can tie into disc-authoring programs from the same manufacturer. Of course this requires your computer to have a Blu-ray drive that can write discs.

A second option is to create a high definition file that you burn onto a regular DVD. You then play the DVD in an advanced DVD player that is capable of playing HD files. Although this is not a common feature on DVD players, there are some out there that can do it. Before Blu-ray burners were available, this was one of the few ways to play back HD content in the field.

Whatever you have to deliver, the more you can control the compression, the better looking the final result will be. It is not uncommon for a file to be compressed more than one time. But while it's not uncommon, that doesn't make it a good practice. Just as when you work with image files, you want to avoid multiple steps of compression.

Movie files can be very big. Longer clips are measured in gigabytes, not megabytes. The file size means longer times to upload, download, archive, and transfer from one location to another.

Glossary

angle of view
The area seen by a lens, usually measured in degrees across the diagonal of the film frame.

aperture
The opening in the lens that allows light to enter the camera. Apertures are usually described as f/numbers. The higher the f/number, the smaller the aperture. The lower the f/number, the larger the aperture.

aperture priority
A type of automatic exposure in which you manually select the aperture and the camera automatically selects the shutter speed.

automatic exposure
When the camera calculates and adjusts the amount of light necessary to properly form an image on the sensor.

automatic focus
When the camera automatically adjusts the focusing ring on the lens to sharply render the subject.

available light
The amount of illumination at a given location. Applies to natural and environmental light sources but not those supplied specifically for photography. Also called existing light or ambient light.

bulb
The shutter speed setting that comes after 30". Allows the shutter to stay open as long as the shutter release is depressed.

color balance
The sensor's interpretation of the actual colors of the subject.

color space
A template for determining appropriate hue, brightness, and color saturation.

compression
Method of reducing file size through removal of superfluous data, as with the JPEG file format.

contrast
The difference in luminance, density, or darkness, between two tones.

dedicated flash
An electronic flash unit that automatically sets the shutter to the proper synchronization speed and usually also activates a signal in the viewfinder that indicates that the flash is fully charged.

depth of field
The image space in front of and behind the plane of focus which appears acceptably sharp in the photograph.

diaphragm
A mechanism that determines the size of the opening that allows light to pass into the camera when taking a photo.

focal length (f)
When the lens is focused on infinity, it is the distance from the optical center of the lens to the focal plane.

focal plane
The plane on which a lens forms a sharp image. Also, the film plane or sensor plane.

f/stop
The size of the aperture or diaphragm opening of a lens. Also referred to as f/number or stop. Stands for the ratio of the focal length (f) of the lens to the width of its aperture opening. (Ex. f/1.4mm = wide opening and f/22mm = narrow opening.) Each stop up (lower f/number) doubles the amount of light reaching

the sensor. Each stop down (higher f/number) halves the amount of light reaching the sensor.

guide number (GN)
A number used to quantify the output of a flash unit. Derived by using this formula: GN = aperture x distance. Guide numbers are expressed in either feet or meters.

histogram
A graphic representation of image tones.

ISO
Traditionally applied to film, this number indicates the relative light sensitivity of the recording medium—the sensor, in this case. Can be adjusted for each shot on the Digital Rebel.

light meter
Also called an exposure meter, it is a device that measures light levels and calculates the correct aperture and shutter speed.

manual exposure
A camera operating mode that allows you to determine and set both the aperture and shutter speed yourself. The opposite of automatic exposure—the mode in which the camera makes these decisions for you.

noise
The digital equivalent of grain. Often caused by sensor or other internal electronic heat. Usually undesirable, but may be added for creative effect using an image-editing program. See also, chrominance and luminance.

RAW
An image file format that has little or no internal processing applied by the camera. Contains 12-bit color information, more complete data than other file formats offer.

resolution

Refers to image quality and clarity, measured in pixels or megapixels. Also, lines per inch on a monitor, or dots per inch on a printed image.

shutter priority

An exposure mode in which you manually select the shutter speed and the camera automatically selects an aperture to match.

single-lens reflex (SLR)

A camera with a mirror that reflects the image entering the lens through a pentaprism onto the viewfinder screen. When you take the picture, the mirror reflexes out of the way, the focal plane shutter opens, and the image is recorded.

standard lens

A fixed-focal-length lens usually in the range of 45 to 55mm. Gives a realistically proportionate perspective of the scene, in contrast to wide-angle or telephoto lenses. Also known as a normal lens.

telephoto lens

A lens with a long focal length that enlarges the subject and produces a narrower angle of view than you would see with your eyes.

wide-angle lens

Produces a greater angle of view than you would see with your eyes, often causing the image to appear stretched. See also, short lens.

zoom lens

A lens that can be adjusted to cover a wide range of focal lengths.

Index

G

H

I

L

M

N

O

P

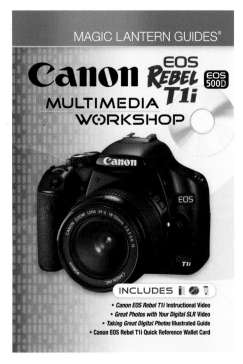
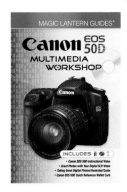
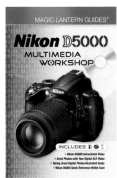
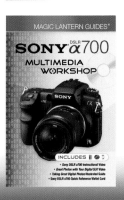